Belgium and France 1914

British Cavalryman

VERSUS

German Cavalryman

Alan Steele

Illustrated by Raffaele Ruggeri

OSPREY PUBLISHING

Bloomsbury Publishing Plc

Kemp House, Chawley Park, Cumnor Hill, Oxford OX2 9PH, UK

29 Earlsfort Terrace, Dublin 2, Ireland

1385 Broadway, 5th Floor, New York, NY 10018, USA

E-mail: info@ospreypublishing.com

www.ospreypublishing.com

OSPREY is a trademark of Osprey Publishing Ltd

First published in Great Britain in 2022

ISBN: PB 9781472848826; eBook 9781472848819; ePDF 9781472848796; XML 9781472848802

22 23 24 25 26   10 9 8 7 6 5 4 3 2 1

Maps by www.bounford.com

Index by Rob Munro

Typeset by PDQ Digital Media Solutions, Bungay, UK

Printed and bound in India by Replika Press Private Ltd.

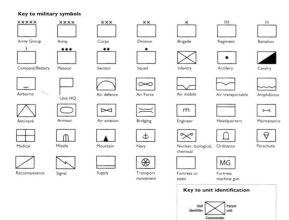

Dedication

I would like to dedicate this book to my nephew Allan Dunbar, Household Cavalry Regiment, descended from a line of soldiers on both sides, but the only true cavalryman in the family.

Acknowledgements

I have the pleasant duty of offering my sincere thanks to the following persons: Benjamin Haas, an independent researcher who on my behalf diligently sought and made copies of relevant war diaries and regimental histories housed in the Bundesarchiv in Freiburg, Germany; Pete Smith, military tour guide and photographer, who visited the battlefields in France, took photographs and cleared up some issues of topography for me; and Aline Staes, Collections Manager of the York Army Museum, who granted me access to copies of the personal diaries of Captain Wright and Private Dyer of the 4th Dragoon Guards. The following curators, archivists and librarians also provided me with helpful information for which I am grateful: Will Bennett and Tony Cowan, the British Commission for Military History; Jacqui Grainger, Librarian of The Royal United Services Institute, London; Lisa Schraut, Bundesarchiv, Abteilung Militärarchiv, Freiburg; Steffi Steffens, Deutsche Nationalbibliothek, Leipzig; Angela Tarnowski, The Royal Lancers Museum, Derby; and Dr. Frank Wernitz, Deutsche Gesellschaft für Heereskunde.

Author's note

There is a paucity of German accounts of combat at small-unit level. This paucity is due to several factors. First, the bombing of Potsdam in 1944 saw the destruction of the bulk of Prussian Army regimental war diaries, although some survived. Fortunately, the *Erinnerungsblatter deutscher Regimenter (Memorabilia of German Regiments)* series of regimental histories, based on the war diaries and other records, was published in the years between the wars and thus preserves much of the matter recorded in the lost war diaries. Unfortunately, the series is incomplete as not all regiments had written their histories before World War II broke out and it became more difficult to publish books deemed non-essential to the Nazi war effort. The second factor leading to the paucity of German accounts was the collapse of the German imperial social order in the turmoil that followed Germany's defeat in 1918. This meant that there was little interest in publishing soldiers' memoirs. Third, such German accounts of the cavalry as have been published, whether in the *Erinnerungsblatter deutscher Regimenter* series or in other semi-official histories or memoirs, are almost invariably written in the spirit of the German romantic tradition. The accounts are highly coloured and impressionistic, but neither precise nor detailed; hence from the German accounts it is often rather difficult to work out where an event occurred or the sequence of events. It is sometimes impossible to reconcile a German account with the British accounts of the same action. In my attempts to reconstruct the small-unit actions described in this book I have sought to collate all of the relevant information derived from both sides. Owing to the limitations of the sources, however, on occasion I have had to make some assumptions or 'best guesses' about the sequence of events and which squadron did what where and when.

Artist's note

CONTENTS

Introduction

In a scene reminiscent of the battle of Waterloo, the infantry stood in close ranks, shoulder to shoulder, their polished leather headgear gleaming in the sunshine. Suddenly, the cavalry was unleashed upon them, charging knee to knee, swarming around the small, isolated clusters of infantrymen, which were destroyed piecemeal. This, however, was 1913, not 1815, and the grand cavalry charge had become the customary concluding exercise to the *Kaisermanöver* of the Imperial German Army. These annual manoeuvres were attended by invited journalists and officers from many foreign nations and served as much to enhance the Kaiser's prestige internationally and to awe other nations with Germany's military might, as they did to actually exercise the German soldiery and staff officers. In 1913 the British military observers were led by Field Marshal Sir John French, who, as Chief of the Imperial General Staff, was Commander-in-Chief of the British Army, and was himself a renowned cavalry leader, having commanded with distinction the British cavalry division during the Second Anglo-Boer War (1899–1902). At the gala to mark the close of the 1913 *Kaisermanöver*, Kaiser Wilhelm II turned to his distinguished British guest and said, 'You have seen how long my sword is; you may find that it is just as sharp!' (quoted in Terraine 1972: 13). A year later, in the opening months of World War I, the Kaiser's bellicose boast was put to the test.

For several decades, the armies of the major industrialized nations of Europe had been sending official observers to study and report on the annual training exercises and actual military operations of each other's armies. Cavalry operations in the American Civil War (1861–65), the Franco-Prussian War (1870–71), the Second Anglo-Boer War and the Russo-Japanese War (1904–05) were minutely analysed, and lessons drawn about the capabilities of, and constraints on, cavalry in modern warfare. For the benefit of their own armies, the attachés translated into their own languages each other's official cavalry training manuals and pamphlets, gave précis of relevant articles on cavalry published in each other's military journals, and made widely available

in translation the books of each other's military theorists. This exchange of ideas and their practical application meant that by 1914 there was broad doctrinal agreement on the wartime role and employment of cavalry among the armies of all the major nations of Europe.

Cavalry and its ancillary arms, such as horse artillery, constituted the only mobile forces available to armies in the early 1900s; aircraft were in their infancy, and neither armoured fighting vehicles nor airmobile troops had even been conceived of. In short, the manoeuvre arm of all armies in 1914 was the cavalry. Owing to its mobility and rapidity of manoeuvre, the cavalry was envisaged as having a threefold strategic and operational role. First, it was to provide an outlying screen to mask and protect its own army so as to prevent the enemy from gaining information about the army's composition, location and movements and, thereby, to deny the enemy intelligence about the commander's intentions. Second, by aggressive and probing reconnaissance it was to penetrate the enemy's outlying cavalry screen in order to ascertain all that information about the enemy's army and intentions that it was trying to deny the enemy about its own forces. Scouting was considered the primary and most important role of the cavalry. At the start of any campaign, therefore, it was anticipated that the cavalry of the opposing forces would inevitably be engaged in combat with each other as they both simultaneously tried to screen their own army and to penetrate the enemy's cavalry screen.

The third cavalry role was, by rapid manoeuvre, to outflank the enemy's forces and threaten to envelop them or to cut their lines of communication, thus forcing them either to offer battle at a disadvantage or to withdraw from a favourable position or even, if completely outmanoeuvred, to surrender without fighting. In addition, the cavalry would spearhead any pursuit of a withdrawing or defeated enemy to harass them, demoralize them and prevent them from rallying and establishing a new defensive position. Implicit in this doctrine of rapid manoeuvre, therefore, was the idea that cavalry could be used to seize points of operational and tactical importance and hold them until the more pedestrian main army could secure them. Likewise, raids against strategic targets in the enemy's hinterland, such as headquarters, supply dumps, railheads, etc., were implied in the concept of rapid manoeuvre. Naturally, the enemy's cavalry, as the only mobile arm they had, would be

ABOVE LEFT
British Army yeomanry on a training exercise at Scole, Norfolk, 7 September 1914. The Yeomanry, as with all of the Territorial Army, were intended for home defence of the UK, but on the outbreak of World War I, volunteered en masse for service overseas with the BEF. (Daily Mirror/ Mirrorpix/Mirrorpix via Getty Images)

ABOVE RIGHT
German hussars launching a mounted attack on the infantry during the *Kaisermanöver*, autumn 1913. The infantry, concentrated in dense formations, can be seen in the distance. (ullstein bild/ullstein bild via Getty Images)

MAP KEY

1 4 August 1914: Höherer Kavallerie-Kommandeur 2, tasked with providing strategic reconnaissance, assembles near Aachen between the 1. Armee and the 2. Armee. When the Germans are delayed at Liège, HKK 2 provides a protective screen around the city.

2 7 August 1914: Höherer Kavallerie-Kommandeur 1 assembles in Luxembourg and advances north-west on Namur, cutting across the advance of the 2. Armee, before swinging south-west to follow the line of the Sambre and Oise rivers towards Maubeuge in France.

3 12 August 1914: After the fall of Liège, HKK 2 continues its advance across Belgium. At the town of Haelen, the 4. Kavallerie-Division attempts to force a crossing of the Gette River, but is repulsed with heavy losses by Belgian forces.

4 16 August 1914: In a manner indicative of the orderly movement of the units of the British Expeditionary Force to their appointed positions, the 4th Dragoon Guards disembarks at Boulogne at about 0630hrs. On 18 August the regiment is moved by train to Hautmont via Amiens; by 21 August it has marched to Harmignies in Belgium; the following day it is in action against the Germans.

5 22 August 1914: Action at Casteau (see pages 28–37).

6 23 August 1914: The battle of Mons. Following skirmishes between German and British cavalry, the 1. Armee runs into the main force of the BEF around the town of Mons. By the end of the day the BEF has been driven back 3 miles (4.8km). Learning that the French V Armée has retreated, thus exposing the BEF's right flank, Field Marshal French orders the BEF to withdraw southwards.

7 24 August 1914: Action at Audregnies. On the morning of 24 August, 5th Division, on II Corps' western flank, encounters the advance elements of the IV. Armeekorps. Brigadier-General Sir Henry de Beauvoir de Lisle's 2nd Cavalry Brigade is ordered to cover 5th Division's flank. Through a series of misunderstandings and unclear orders, the 4th Dragoon Guards and the 9th Lancers charge in column of squadrons across 1,200yd (1.1km) of open fields. In the face of heavy fire the two regiments do not reach the German lines but retire in disorder, suffering 169 casualties and losing over 300 horses between them.

8 26 August 1914: The battle of Le Cateau. General Sir Horace Smith-Dorrien's II Corps, supported by the Cavalry Division and a French cavalry corps, turns and faces the 1. Armee, but Lieutenant-General Sir Douglas Haig's I Corps continues its southwards withdrawal. Outnumbered and facing encirclement, II Corps carries out a fighting withdrawal.

9 28 August 1914: Action at Cerizy–Moÿ (see pages 38–53).

10 1 September 1914: Action at Néry. After launching a surprise attack on the 1st Cavalry Brigade at Néry, the 4. Kavallerie-Division is forced to retire in some disorder, abandoning all of its artillery and losing about 180 men and 232 horses killed, wounded, missing or captured. The 1st Cavalry Brigade suffers 42 men killed and 92 wounded and loses about 380 horses.

11 7 September 1914: Action at Le Montcel (see pages 54–70).

trying to counter any enveloping movement by one's own cavalry while attempting to outmanoeuvre one's own forces in the same manner. Once again, it was anticipated that this would lead to mounted combat between the opposing cavalry forces.

While there was, thus, broad agreement about the strategic and operational roles of cavalry there was less agreement about how cavalry should fulfil these roles at the tactical level. It was clear that, whether on the offensive or defensive strategically or operationally, cavalry would almost always be required to be tactically offensive in order to thwart or defeat the enemy's cavalry. Cavalry formations in all armies were essentially the line abreast for attack and the column for manoeuvre, or various combinations of these two. Debates about cavalry tactics, therefore, tended to focus on what was the best weaponry with which to equip the cavalry of a modern army, in order to defeat enemy cavalry most decisively, while at the same time allowing the cavalry to operate effectively against enemy infantry and artillery.

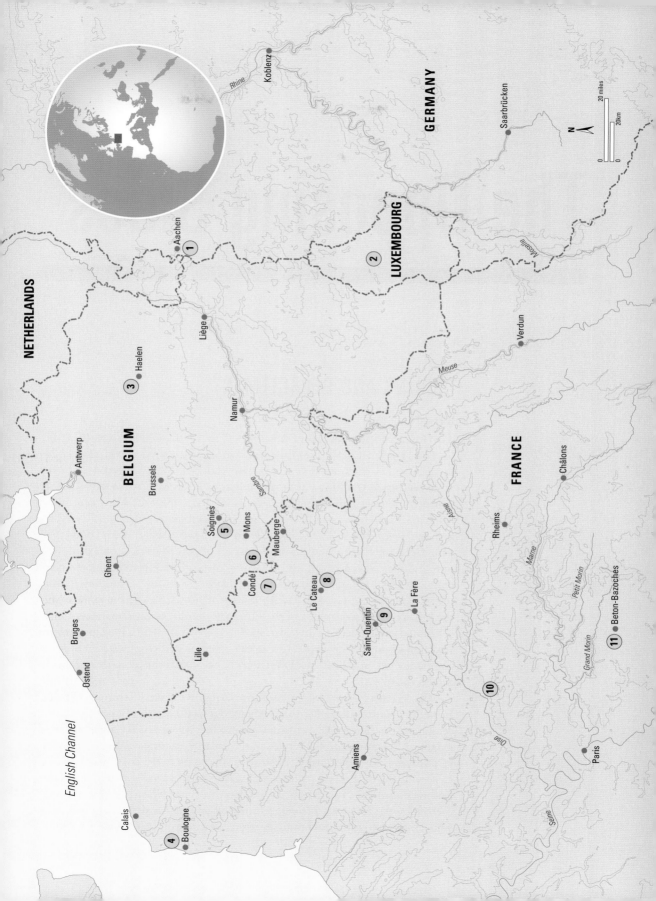

English Channel

NETHERLANDS

BELGIUM

GERMANY

LUXEMBOURG

FRANCE

Koblenz

Rhine

Saarbrücken

Aachen **1**

2

Moselle

Liège

Verdun

Haelen

3

Meuse

Namur

Antwerp

Brussels

Châlons

Sambre

Soignies **5** Mons

Rheims

Maubege

6

Aisne

Ghent

Condé **7**

Le Cateau **8**

La Fère

Marne

Beton-Bazoches **11**

Saint-Quentin **9**

Petit Morin

Bruges

Lille

Grand Morin

Ostend

10

Oise

Amiens

Paris

Calais

4 Boulogne

Seine

N

20 miles

20km

0

0

The Opposing Sides

ORIGINS AND RECRUITMENT

German

The Imperial German Army was formed in 1871 on the creation of the Second German Empire from the unification of a confederation of over 20 independent German states under Prussian leadership. The new army inherited a host of proud traditions from the militaries of these German states, all of which could trace continuous histories of service going back many centuries, from the Franco-Prussian War through the Napoleonic Wars (1796–1815) and the Seven Years' War (1756–63) to the Thirty Years' War (1618–48). Among German cavalry officers, almost all of whom were drawn from the nobility, there was a strong emphasis on chivalrous mounted combat. This emphasis was imparted to the rank-and-file troopers during training by the celebration of great German cavalry leaders of yore. Cavalrymen were taught the history and past exploits of the different German cavalry regiments, and celebrated cavalry actions. In short, the German cavalry had a long and proud tradition of exemplary service in war and an ethos that emphasized mounted combat, whether against enemy infantry or cavalry, as the pinnacle of cavalry achievement.

The German Army was a conscript army, with recruits mostly drawn from the countryside and with an average age of 20 at call-up. Owing to the prolonged time required – two years – to produce fully trained cavalrymen, the length of full-time national service in the cavalry was three years, as opposed to two years for other arms. Thereafter there was a 4½-year commitment to service in the Reserve, after which cavalrymen served in the Landwehr (militia) until they turned 45. In addition to those who were conscripted, there were the *Einjährig-Freiwilliger*, men with a higher degree of education who volunteered for a year's military service in a unit of their choice. Owing to

During the Franco-Prussian War, Generalmajor Ferdinand von Bredow led Kürassier-Regiment 7 and Ulanen-Regiment 16 in what became known as the *Todesritt* ('death ride') against French infantry and artillery at Vionville during the battle of Mars-la-Tour on 16 August 1870. The two regiments suffered almost 50 per cent casualties in the charge, but it became a celebrated episode in German cavalry history. The German cavalry held commemorative services on 16 August 1914 during the advance through Belgium and the *Todesritt* was frequently referenced by German cavalry commanders as a model of the selfless sacrifice to which cavalrymen should aspire. (Getty Images/clu)

the cavalry's prestige, there were always enough volunteers for the arm, which, therefore, did not struggle to recruit sufficient NCOs, unlike the other arms.

Imperial German Army cavalry regiments bore designations that in some cases dated back centuries. Here, uhlans (lancers) participate in an exercise in 1884, at which time only units designated as uhlans carried lances. In 1890, all German cavalry regiments were re-armed with the *Stahlrohrlanze* ('steel-tube lance'). (Ludwig Boedecker/ullstein bild via Getty Images)

Published in 1900, this illustration depicts the 21st Lancers charging in the battle of Omdurman, 2 September 1898, during the British conquest of the Sudan. This charge, mounted by some 320 men against an unshaken force of over 1,700 Dervish infantry, was one of the most celebrated British cavalry actions in 'the small wars of empire'. The lancers managed to fight their way through the Dervish infantry, in the process suffering 21 men killed and 50 wounded, with 119 horses killed or wounded, but without shaking or dispersing the enemy. It was only when the lancers dismounted and opened fire with their carbines that the Dervishes withdrew. Within 18 months of this famous charge, the British cavalry and yeomanry operating in South Africa during the Second Anglo-Boer War were using very different tactics, having been forced to adopt the methods of their Boer adversaries who were essentially mounted riflemen. (Universal History Archive/ Universal Images Group via Getty Images)

British

The British cavalry also had a long and admirable history, stretching back to the time of the Civil Wars between the Crown and Parliament (1638–60). In the European wars of the 1700s and 1800s the British cavalry, although gallant and often effective, gained a reputation for impetuously 'galloping at everything'. Throughout the 19th century, however, the British cavalry found itself opposed to a variety of foes in the small wars of empire, and it had to be flexible in the application of tactics to be able to operate effectively against a wide variety of enemies from Zulus in Africa to Sikhs in India.

The most salutary lessons for the British cavalry came during the Second Anglo-Boer War when they were opposed by a highly mobile force of mounted riflemen who ran rings around them. It became apparent how poor the troops were at scouting – a traditional cavalry role – as compared with the Boers. Moreover, the British cavalry found very few opportunities for shock action and, as the war progressed, they were compelled to adopt Boer tactics as mounted riflemen. Furthermore, British cavalry horsemastership was shown to be execrable, with thousands of horses dying or being rendered ineffective through saddle sores. By the end of the war in 1902, the reputation of the British cavalry was very low (Barrow 1942: 111*f*). Their horsemastership was appalling, their weapons were ineffective and their ability to provide timely intelligence about the enemy was non-existent. Amid calls for wholesale reform, there were even some who called for the complete disbandment of the cavalry and the creation of a force of mounted riflemen in its stead (Badsey 2008: 143*ff*). This particular threat was averted, but the message was clear: the days of the enthusiastic impetuous amateur 'Cavalier' were over; the time of the sober professional cavalryman had come.

The British Army did not take conscripts but enlisted volunteers who, in the cavalry, served a minimum of seven years in the Regular Army, followed by five in the Reserve after leaving the Regulars (Maitland 1951: 119). The majority of recruits were townsmen, and few had any experience or knowledge of horses until they joined the cavalry (Van Emden 1996: 21).

WEAPONS AND TACTICS

German

At the beginning of the 20th century cavalry officers across Europe were engaged in a fierce debate as to the primary tactical function of cavalry in war and, depending on what this was deemed to be, the primary weapon with which cavalry should be equipped. For the German cavalry the decision about its primary weapon, and, therefore, its primary tactical function, was resolved in 1890 when all German cavalry regiments, irrespective of their traditional role and armament, were equipped with the new *Stahlrohrlanze*. As a secondary weapon the cavalryman also had a straight-bladed sword, the Modell 1889 *Kavalleriedegen* or, if a cuirassier, the Modell 1883 *Pallasch*.

The standard firearm of the German cavalry in 1914 was the 7.92mm-calibre Mauser Karabiner 98AZ (Kar 98AZ), which was introduced as a shortened carbine version of the standard infantry rifle in 1908. Some Reserve cavalry units were still issued with the even shorter and older cavalry carbine first introduced in 1898 and, confusingly, also designated the Karabiner 98. The Kar 98AZ was an effective and accurate weapon, but the general standard of musketry in the German Army as a whole was not high. The Germans did not teach their infantry to shoot at ranges over 400m (437yd) and only officers were taught to judge distances and indicate targets. Rapid fire for the Germans was 8–9rd/min and not all soldiers were trained to that standard (Creagh 1915: vii). This poor standard of musketry was even lower in the cavalry as weapon-handling training emphasized the use of the lance in mounted combat over the carbine in dismounted combat (Poseck 1921: 216f). The *Exerzier-Reglement für die Kavallerie 1909* (§12) stipulated that, 'The cavalry should always seek to solve their tasks offensively. Only when the lance is out of place does one reach for the carbine. No squadron should wait to be attacked but should always attack the enemy first.' Admittedly, the 1909 Regulations gave the same amount of space to dismounted combat

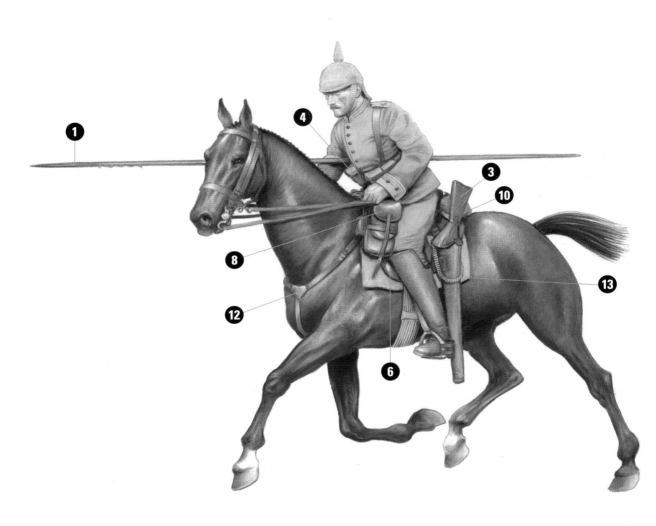

This *Kürassier* has been campaigning and fighting for some three weeks now and, therefore, both he and his horse are rather jaded from long marches in high summer temperatures and periodic soakings from thunderstorms, as well as from weeks of bivouacking in the fields. Added to this is the strain of constant scouting in hostile territory, searching for the Allied forces, and of being subjected to repeated guerrilla attacks by Belgian *francs tireurs*.

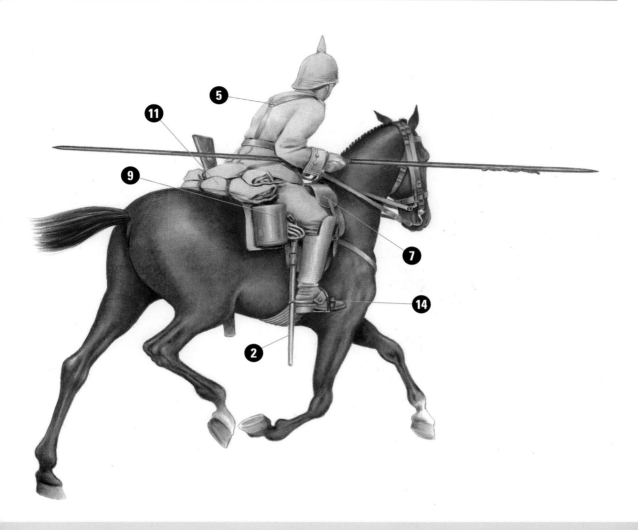

Weapons, dress and equipment

In 1914 the German cavalryman carried the *Stahlrohrlanze* (**1**) as his primary weapon. As this man is a *Kürassier* he carries the heavy cavalry Modell 1883 *Pallasch* (**2**) rather than the standard Modell 1889 *Kavalleriedegen.* In its bucket is his 7.92mm Mauser Karabiner 98AZ carbine (**3**), which was shorter than the standard infantry rifle.

As a cuirassier he wears the Modell 1894 *Pickelhaube*, which had a 'lobster-tail' extension at the back, and riding boots with a high knee-flap. His tunic is the standard cavalry *Waffenrock* worn by cuirassiers and dragoons. On the front of his belt, he has six ammunition pouches (**4**), each holding four five-round ammunition clips for his carbine, making 120 rounds in total. The weight of the belt is supported by a leather Y-pattern yoke (**5**) over his shoulders. At some point he has lost his aluminium water bottle, which would normally be clipped to his belt.

He is seated on the Armeesattel 89 saddle (**6**). Over the pommel are hung two saddle wallets (**7**), into which he has stuffed all his personal effects, such as washing kit, pipe, spare socks, etc., as well as the kit for grooming and cleaning his horse. The nearside wallet has a horseshoe case (**8**) attached, which held spare horseshoes and nails. Attached to the cantle is his mess tin (**9**) and 24 hours' rations in a brown leather case on the offside, and a canvas fodder bag (**10**), which normally hung behind the rifle bucket; owing to resupply difficulties it is empty, so it is folded against the bedding roll (**11**) inside a waterproof groundsheet. The horse has a leather breastplate (**12**). Suspended from the rifle bucket is the heel rope (**13**) to tether the horse. Attached to each stirrup is a small leather lance bucket (**14**), into which the butt of the lance could be placed to support the weight of the lance when on the march.

A German cavalry communications detachment lays telephone cable during a training exercise, 1910. Robust and portable communications systems are a vital part of any military organization, but telephone and radio communication were in their infancy in 1914. The British cavalry relied exclusively on despatch riders and signallers trained in visual signalling by semaphore or Morse lamp. The German cavalry, however, included a telephone detachment with each cavalry division as well as portable radios. The radios were sensitive and required time to set up in order to transmit. Nevertheless, German cavalry reconnaissance patrols in the early days of the campaign would sometimes take radios with them in order to send signals back to divisional headquarters. In this, they were far ahead of the Allied cavalry. (ullstein bild/ullstein bild via Getty Images)

as they did to mounted combat and placed less emphasis on frontal attacks by whole divisions of cavalry and more on flanking attacks by squadrons, but in practice the cavalry only paid lip-service to dismounted combat. German cavalry tactics, therefore, still focused on the mounted charge despite recognition by some cavalrymen that modern firepower made such charges impracticable (Satter 2004: 30*f*). Recognizing that the cavalry had inadequate firepower, the German Army experimented with attaching *Jäger* battalions to cavalry divisions during the *Kaisermanöver* of 1913. The *Jäger* were light infantry trained in rapid movement, skirmishing and sharpshooting. Moreover, each *Jäger* battalion had a machine-gun detachment, which the cavalry regiments lacked. This combination of cavalry and *Jäger* worked well and was implemented in the campaign of 1914.

A German cavalry patrol, showing the standard German cavalry practice of pegging lances upright into the ground whenever they dismounted. (Historic Collection/Alamy Stock Photo)

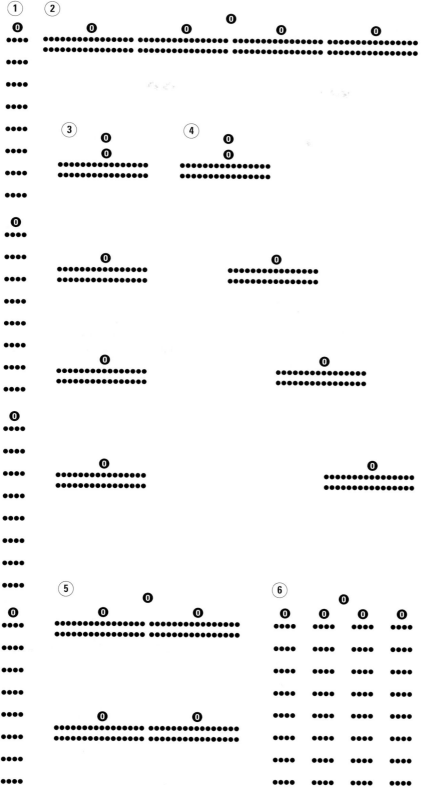

In 1914 cavalry squadrons of all armies employed six basic formations to manoeuvre. In these diagrams officers, whether squadron or troop commanders, are indicated by 'O'. The squadron in column of sections (**1**), which was the standard marching formation, had each troop in column of sections formation, one behind another in file. The squadron in line (**2**) was the standard attack formation with the four troops in line side-by-side without any interval between troops. The squadron column (**3**) was the usual manoeuvre formation in the face of the enemy. The troops were each in line one behind another, but with sufficient interval between them that a wheel left or right would bring the squadron into line. The squadron half-column (**4**) was an interim manoeuvre formation when a squadron had made a half-wheel from either line or squadron column. The column of half-squadrons (**5**) allowed the squadron to deploy for an attack when its frontage was constricted for any reason. The interval between the two lines of troops was the same as the frontage of a troop in line, thus allowing the squadron to wheel right or left and remain in column of half-squadrons. The line of troop columns (**6**) had each troop in 'column of sections'. The troops were parallel to each other side-by-side at sufficient interval to allow a squadron line to be formed promptly. This formation was useful for manoeuvring over broken terrain.

At this early stage of the campaign — the BEF had been in France only about a week — the British cavalryman is conforming to regulation marching order uniform and equipment. Everything was designed to minimize weight and for utility and there were regular inspections to ensure that the men were not carrying any extra weight in terms of personal effects. Doubtless, however, the ingenuity of the soldiers and the leniency of the NCOs meant that small personal items were carried.

Weapons, dress and equipment

This private is armed with the Pattern 1908 Cavalry Sword (**1**), which he is holding at the 'point'. Hanging from the near side of the saddle is the steel sword scabbard (**2**). He also has the .303in SMLE bolt-action rifle (**3**), inserted in its leather bucket, which he was trained to use to the same high standard as the infantry.

He wears a khaki jacket, riding breeches reinforced with leather at the seat, and puttees. Over his left shoulder he wears the nine-pouch leather bandolier (**4**), which held 90 rounds of ammunition for the rifle. Tucked under the bandolier is his enamelled metal water bottle (**5**). Attached to the outside of the rifle bucket is his aluminium mess tin (**6**). In the haversack (**7**) tucked under his left arm, he carries personal washing kit; spare socks and boot laces; knife, fork and spoon; dubbin and boot brush; an issue notebook and pencil; and one day's rations. In his right pocket is a clasp-knife, attached to his arm by a lanyard.

Attached to the front offside of his saddle is a horseshoe pouch (**8**) with spare horseshoe and nails. Over the front arch of the saddle is a rolled-up groundsheet (**9**) inside which is a folded mackintosh for wet weather, and a rubber and sponge for cleaning the horse. Suspended from the rear nearside of the saddle is the feed bag (**10**) with a day's rations for the horse, plus the curry comb and body brush. Beneath the feed bag, attached to the scabbard are two picketing pegs (**11**) and a wooden mallet. Around the horse's neck is the heel rope (**12**) by which the horse is tethered in camp. Attached to this is usually a section of 'built-up' rope for making picketing lines for the horses when in bivouac, but this private seems to have mislaid his since arriving in France. Finally, the man is sitting in the steel-arched 1912 Universal Pattern saddle (**13**), which proved to be one of the best cavalry saddles ever designed.

British

In the British Army, too, there was a fierce debate about the correct weapons and tactical role of cavalry, started in 1903 by the Commander-in-Chief, Lord Roberts, himself. He argued that the cavalry should be equally capable of operating dismounted as well as mounted and should be equally proficient with the rifle as with the *arme blanche* and, regarding the latter, that the sword was preferable to the lance, which was to be withdrawn from service. The main points of his argument were subsequently proved correct, but it sparked years of acrimonious and public debate (Badsey 2008: 143*ff*).

Uniformity of cavalry doctrine was finally achieved in 1912 with the publication of *Cavalry Training 1912* for the British Army's regular cavalry, and a simplified version, *Yeomanry and Mounted Rifle Training 1912*, for the Yeomanry in Britain and the colonial forces of the Dominions. The new doctrine stipulated that cavalry could often achieve the best results by a combination of both dismounted rifle fire and mounted shock action. Emphasis was also placed on cooperation with other arms, particularly artillery and machine guns. In such a combined attack it was stressed that the timing of the fire and shock action must be correct, so that the enemy had no opportunity to recover from the one before being subjected to the other. This also entailed that the two methods of attack did not hinder one another, with the mounted troops not masking the fire support nor the fire support preventing the mounted troops from charging the enemy. It was, therefore, advised that one or both methods of attack should be delivered from the flanks (*Cavalry Training 1912*: §194).

In terms of weapons, therefore, this meant that the cavalry had to be equipped with a new rifle and a new sword – the lance only being reintroduced in 1912. The rifle was the famous .303in SMLE No. 1 Mk III, which entered service in 1907. The new sword was introduced in 1908. It was designed primarily as a thrusting weapon and, hence, the blade was long, straight, and tapered to a point. The front edge was sharpened, but it was not really intended to be used as a cutting blade. The cavalryman was trained to lean forward in the saddle and point the sword with his arm extended in order to

Troops of the British 2nd Cavalry Division pictured alongside a French Army cyclist after crossing the Marne River, September 1914. The French cyclist appears to be a dragoon, indicating that he has lost the use of his horse. French horsemastership was appalling and within a short time of the outbreak of World War I, large numbers of French remounts were rendered unfit for service due to saddle sores caused by the French cavalry practice of never dismounting, even when at the halt. The British cavalry, by contrast, stressed the importance of dismounting at every opportunity, in order to save the horses. This photo shows British cavalrymen doing just that. (Mirrorpix/Mirrorpix via Getty Images)

Members of a British Army machine-gun section are depicted during training, December 1914. By the standards of 1914, the British cavalry were well supplied with machine guns, each regiment having its own integral machine-gun section with two Maxims. British doctrine also encouraged the cavalry to combine rifle and machine-gun fire with a mounted attack, which the 2nd Dragoons (The Royal Scots Greys) and the 12th Lancers did very effectively at Cerizy–Moÿ. (Bettmann/Getty Images)

lengthen as far as possible his reach with the sword-point. The force to drive home the sword-point was given by the momentum of his galloping horse, not by the cavalryman's own arm muscles, which simply held the blade at the point (*Cavalry Training 1912*: §82). This approach to cavalry swordsmanship was novel and generated some discussion as to its efficacy, as some cavalrymen preferred a curved-bladed cutting sabre. In 1912 an Officers' Cavalry Sword was introduced, designed along similar lines to the Pattern 1908 Cavalry Sword, but it was not as robust a weapon. It was not popular, therefore, and in mounted combat during the war many officers chose to use a different model of sword or a pistol instead of the Pattern 1912 Sword.

TRAINING

Fully trained cavalry was an expensive arm to maintain as it required specially trained men and horses – called 'remounts' in the cavalry – as well as specially designed weapons and equipment, and the development of its own peculiar tactics. Consequently, the training of cavalrymen took considerably longer than that of the infantry or other arms.

Equitation, the training of both horse and rider, is training in the 'aids' by which the rider communicates his intentions to the horse so that it understands what is required. These aids consist of gentle pressure on the horse's mouth by means of the bit and reins, and subtle pressure on the horse's back and flanks by squeezing with the legs and shifting the weight in the saddle. By these means the rider directs the horse's movement and paces. The rider's hold on the reins is, therefore, a crucial aid in equitation. Unlike a civilian rider who holds the reins with both hands, the cavalryman had to be trained to ride with the reins threaded through the fingers of his left hand so that by slight flexions of the wrist he could control and direct the horse while wielding a weapon in his right hand. Cavalrymen, therefore, had to be trained to have a light touch on the reins or they could permanently ruin a horse's mouth, making it unresponsive to pressure on the bit and, therefore, useless as a cavalry remount. The rider's 'seat' – how he sits in the saddle – is also important as it determines both his own balance and that of the horse. A rider with an insecure seat will struggle to remain in the saddle and will hinder the natural movements of the horse. Moreover, a rider with a bad seat will not be able to use the aids effectively. In 1914 the style of equitation was very different from the present-day 'Forward Seat', which was first proposed by Capitano Federico Caprilli of the Italian Army in the early 1900s and which helps the horse to stay balanced and collected. In 1914 neither the German nor the British cavalry used the 'Forward Seat'.

Horsemastership is training the rider to care for his horse, whether in the field or stables, in order to keep the horse healthy and fit. It entails understanding the watering and feeding of horses; their daily grooming; shoeing; veterinary first aid for minor injuries and diseases; and the proper fitting of saddlery, so as to prevent discomfort or injury to the horse. A cavalry force whose soldiers are trained horsemasters will be able to reduce wastage of horseflesh on campaign by keeping the greatest number of remounts healthy and fit for active service duties.

Drill entailed training both soldiers and remounts to form up in organized bodies and to move in ranks and columns, to change from one formation to another in an orderly way, to change direction as a formed body of cavalry quickly and efficiently, and to move as a formed body at a standard speed, which allowed ground to be covered quickly but without the cavalry formation losing cohesion. Drill was, therefore, the foundation on which collective training was built and it taught cavalrymen automatically to adopt those formations that allowed cavalry squadrons to manoeuvre effectively on the battlefield in the face of the enemy.

German

The annual intake was in the spring and the recruits were assigned to their respective regiments for initial training in drill and physical fitness. The annual special-to-arm training cycle began on 1 October every year when the conscripts were assigned to squadrons, making up about one-third of the numbers in each squadron, and concluding with the *Kaisermanöver* the following year. Hence two-thirds of the German Army was already fully trained at the start of the training cycle. Coincidentally, this also meant that the whole German Army was fully trained and at peak readiness when World War I broke out in 1914. Cavalry special-to-arm training consisted of equitation, weapon-handling, close order drill for massed cavalry manoeuvre, and minor tactics, such as patrolling and scouting (Pelet-Narbonne 1911: *passim*; Satter 2004: 28f; Unger 1912: *passim*). Reconnaissance was largely carried out by officers' patrols, though not very efficiently according to the British (Vaughan 1954: 163; Watson 2016: 40).

The German cavalry in 1914 were influenced by *Haute École* schooling in dressage. This meant that their horses were very well trained and obedient, as British cavalry officers noted when German remounts were captured in 1914. The German regulation cavalry seat taught the rider to sit erect and forward in the saddle with the heel of his boot in the stirrup lined up beneath

his centre of gravity, thus ensuring both balance and stability in the saddle. In this it was close to the 'Forward Seat' except in the prescribed posture when descending slopes or jumping obstacles, in which the rider was taught to lean right back in the saddle, whereas nowadays the rider is taught to rise from the saddle, taking his weight on his knees, and to lean forward over the horse's neck. One disadvantage of dressage, however, is that the horse's head is pulled down to create a graceful curve of the neck, thus preventing the horse from seeing where it is going as it is looking just in front of its feet rather than ahead as it would if its head and neck were extended naturally. This unnatural posture is clearly seen in the illustration of the *Richtiger Sitz* ('correct seat') in the German equitation manual (*Reitvorschrift 1912*: 45). So, while German cavalrymen and remounts were well schooled in the *manège*, they were, perhaps, less confident in cross-country riding in which the horse had to be allowed some freedom to look ahead and place its own feet to avoid any irregularities in the ground surface.

German cavalry horsemastership was excellent in stables, but with no recent experience of campaigning, the Germans found it difficult to maintain proper care of their remounts in the field. They had to learn the hard way how to maintain the health and fitness of their remounts when living out-of-doors on short rations and under a heavy workload. The losses in horseflesh during the first month of World War I, well over 50 per cent in some cavalry regiments, was the price paid to acquire that knowledge.

British

Once a volunteer recruit had passed his medical examination, he was sent to a depot for three months of basic training, which – like the German – consisted largely of drill and physical instruction. When a recruit had successfully completed this he joined his regiment, was assigned to a squadron, and by attendance at the obligatory 'stables' each morning and evening was taught how to care for his horse efficiently and effectively. He also began to learn military equitation. This course could last up to nine months, depending on the prior experience and ability of the soldier. Weapon-handling of both *arme blanche* and rifle was also taught. Initially, sword or lance drill was learned on foot, but once he was a proficient rider, the cavalryman learned

ABOVE LEFT
Garde-Dragoner practise lance drill on foot, 1905. All weapon-handling training was initially conducted on foot until the recruits had thoroughly mastered the different movements necessary to wield the weapon well. Once they were proficient on foot, the recruits progressed to carrying out the exercise on horseback, which brought its own challenges. By the end of their second year of training the recruits could be considered proficient cavalrymen. (ullstein bild/ullstein bild via Getty Images)

ABOVE RIGHT
Troops of the 2. Kavallerie-Division jump a fence during training. Notice how all of them are leaning right back in the saddle and pulling on the horses' mouths; a practice that would not be tolerated nowadays. (ullstein bild/ullstein bild via Getty Images)

ABOVE LEFT
A British cavalry scout, November 1914. (Mirrorpix/Mirrorpix via Getty Images)

ABOVE RIGHT
British cavalry march dismounted beside their horses, France, 1914. As a fundamental part of being a good horsemaster, the British cavalryman was trained to spare his horse as much as he could and to dismount whenever at the halt. In addition, it was common practice for the men to dismount periodically and march alongside their horses in order to rest them and prevent saddle sores. The British cavalry probably had the best horsemastership of any European cavalry throughout World War I. (The Print Collector/Print Collector/Getty Images)

weapon-handling while mounted. This individual training culminated with collective training in minor tactics, scouting, etc., in the summer, building up from troop and squadron training in July to regimental and brigade training in August. Thus, as with the German Army, the outbreak of World War I found the British Army fully trained (Maitland 1951: *passim*; Van Emden 1996: 11–29).

In the British cavalry recruits normally took nine months to pass out of the riding school (Van Emden 1996: 21). They were taught to use what was known as 'The Hunting Seat'; i.e. the style commonly used in riding to hounds on the hunting field. In 1914 this entailed sitting well down in the saddle on one's buttocks with a slightly bent leg, gripping largely with the thighs, and with the heel of the boot well in front of the rider's centre of gravity. In its more extreme form, it was an ungainly seat, and an American officer who taught equitation to the US cavalry called the British hunting seat 'grotesque' (Felton 1962: 49); but it was also an effective seat for cross-country riding, as proven by its use on both the hunting field and in mounted combat. It is noteworthy that the British cavalry did not substantially change its method of equitation between the Second Anglo-Boer War and World War II. What it did change, however, after its humiliating experience against the Boers, was its horsemastership.

In 1914 the British cavalry probably had the best horsemasters of any cavalry in the world. The British cavalryman was taught to see his horse as his best friend and to consider its needs before his own. He was trained to dismount whenever the unit halted on the march and, also, periodically to march on foot beside his horses so as to ease the pressure on the horse's back; a practice that astonished the French cavalry. In addition, British cavalrymen sought opportunities to look after their remounts, whether by simply loosening the girths whenever there was the chance or by gathering grain to feed the horses from the numerous corn stooks dotting the fields (Coleman 1916: 12; Barrow 1942: 147). Attention to small details such as this meant that British cavalry remounts stayed in better condition for longer than those of either the German or the French cavalries.

MOBILIZATION, LOGISTICS AND MORALE

German

The Schlieffen Plan (Germany's operational plan for the attack on France and Russia) had some noteworthy logistical implications for the German cavalry. First, that the maximum possible number of German mobile troops, i.e. cavalry and *Jäger*, should be placed with the right wing of the German Army, as it was this wing which would be required rapidly to carry out the wide swing through Belgium into north-western France. The Germans allocated four cavalry corps designated *Höherer Kavallerie-Kommandeure* (HKK: 'Higher Cavalry Commanders') to the Western Front, but only two of these were assigned to the right wing: Generalleutnant Freiherr Manfred von Richthofen's HKK 1 (the Garde-Kavallerie-Division and the 5. Kavallerie-Division) and Generalleutnant Georg von der Marwitz's HKK 2 (the 2., 4. and 9. Kavallerie-Divisionen). The other two cavalry corps were allocated to those parts of the German Army which, under the Schlieffen Plan, were intended to remain static or, even, to pull back in order to draw in the French: HKK 4 was assigned to the centre and HKK 3 to the left wing in Lorraine. Moreover, the forested and mountainous terrain of the Ardennes and Vosges *départements* on these fronts was not conducive to large-scale cavalry operations.

In the event, HKK 4, in attempting a strategic reconnaissance in force, was unable to penetrate the French defences and advanced no more than 15 miles (24km) from its assembly areas before it was rebuffed. Likewise, HKK 3's strategic reconnaissance petered out without producing the desired results and on 14 August it was ordered by Generaloberst Graf Helmuth von Moltke, Chief of the General Staff, to pull back behind the infantry corps holding the common frontier with France (Humphries & Maker 2013: 110–12). As reconnaissance was the primary role of cavalry, this failure to carry it out was a somewhat disheartening and chastening experience for the German cavalry. There is, thus, some justification for the view that these cavalry corps would have been better employed with the right wing of the

The 2. Garde-Kürassier-Regiment, part of the Garde-Kavallerie-Division, is cheered by crowds of civilians as it leaves Berlin for the front, August 1914. (Interim Archives/Getty Images)

A remount inspection in Hamburg, August 1914. With the outbreak of World War I, horses were requisitioned or purchased from civilian sources, to bring the cavalry up to full establishment. Each horse had to be checked over by cavalry officers and veterinarians to ensure it was suitable for cavalry service. (ullstein bild/ullstein bild via Getty Images)

German armies in its advance through Belgium (Poseck 1921: 210–11). It is difficult to see, however, how room would have been found for four cavalry corps to advance through Belgium when the logistics of moving the 1. and 2. Armeen and HKK 1 and 2 were already immensely complex. As it was, there was only room for HKK 1 to assemble in southern Luxembourg, so that it then had to march north-west across the path of the 2. Armee in order to advance on Namur.

Another unanticipated logistical implication of the Schlieffen Plan was the physical demands made on both horses and men in the right wing of the German Army by the rapid and lengthy march across Belgium and France. For example, between 4 August and 8 September, Ulanen-Regiment 5 marched 438 miles (705km), averaging 24 miles (39km) per day, with the shortest day's march being 9 miles (14km) and the longest 38½ miles (62km) (Westecker 1939: 113). One effect of these long marches on the hard paved roads was that horseshoes wore out more quickly than they could be replaced (Poseck 1921: 214). In addition, the weather in August 1914 was unusually hot and sunny, interspersed with heavy downpours and thunderstorms, which produced its own fatigue and proved especially wearing for the horses, which were used to living in sheltered stables. Moreover, the Germans were unable to maintain a regular supply of oats to the cavalry, the first shortages occurring within two days of crossing into Belgium, causing the horses further to lose condition (Poseck 1921: 12; Humphries & Maker 2013: 108). Losses in horseflesh were, therefore, high. For example, after a month of campaigning, Kürassier-Regiment 4 was reduced from 180 trained remounts per squadron to 60–80, the shortfall being made up by requisitioning untrained civilian horses or by putting horseless cavalrymen onto bicycles (Westecker 1939: 105). The attached *Jäger* battalions also found these long daily marches hard going, even with bicycles and lorry transport, the men often sleeping on the ground in the open as, by evening, they were too tired to put up their tents (Müller 1922: 13).

For the Germans the invasion of Belgium was simply a strategic necessity to outflank the French Army and to allow Paris to be invested. In their

A *Zug* from the 1. Garde-Dragoner-Regiment preparing for mounted drill with the lance. The ideal which all German cavalrymen were taught to aspire to was that of chivalrous mounted combat between two opposing cavalry forces. Unfortunately, this ideal crumbled in the face of guerrilla warfare by Belgian *franc tireurs* and costly mounted assaults against foes armed with modern firearms. (ullstein bild/ullstein bild via Getty Images)

planning the Germans do not seem to have anticipated the strong resistance put up by the Belgians, which caused further attrition on man and beast from casualties and by prolonging the time taken for the Germans to reach the French frontier. The first unwelcome surprise the Germans received was the ubiquitous presence of Belgian *franc tireurs* ('free shooters'; irregular fighters). The cavalry, advancing in small, isolated patrols to reconnoitre, was particularly vulnerable to ambush or sniping by these armed civilians and began to suffer casualties before it had even encountered the Belgian Army. The German response was severe; any civilian found with a weapon was summarily executed and buildings from which shots had been fired were burned to the ground (Poseck 1921: 10–11). These reprisals were hardly in accord with the ideal of chivalrous mounted combat with which the German cavalry had been imbued and carrying them out undoubtedly had a demoralizing effect (in both meanings of the word) on the German cavalrymen.

On 12 August German cavalry morale received a further blow when the 4. Kavallerie-Division experienced a chastening reverse at the hands of the despised Belgian cavalry in the battle of Haelen. In accordance with their pre-war training, doctrine and ethos, the division delivered repeated but piecemeal squadron charges against the Belgian cavalry, which had dismounted and formed firing lines along hedgerows. The German cavalry were repulsed with heavy losses, suffering total casualties of 492 men and 843 horses, as compared with Belgian casualties of 127 men and 100 horses (Satter 2004: 97). It was a sobering lesson in the effect of modern rifle and machine-gun fire on massed mounted cavalry formations and in the futility of attacking with the lance defenders equipped with modern rifles (Poseck 1921: 26).

British

The logistics of transporting the BEF (British Expeditionary Force) across to France were complex, but everything had been planned down to the smallest detail. The bulk of the BEF had arrived in France by 16 August, and by 21 August the BEF had assembled at Mons in Belgium on the left flank of the French V Armée in accordance with Plan XVII, the French strategic plan for opposing a German invasion – a remarkable feat.

During the retreat from Mons the British were faced with the logistical nightmare of how to keep men and horses resupplied when unit locations were unknown and constantly changing as the BEF withdrew southwards. The regulation daily food ration of the Cavalry Division (9,897 men and 10,195 horses) was 6⅔ tons of meat, 5½ tons of bread and 2⅕ tons of fresh vegetables for the men, and 54½ tons of oats and the same amount of hay for the horses (*Field Service Pocket Book 1913*). The BEF's Quartermaster-General, Major-General Sir William Robertson, had the Army Service Corps stockpile supplies at all major road junctions ahead of the retreating troops, who could then replenish themselves whenever they came across a stockpile. The improvised system worked brilliantly, and an unanticipated benefit was that the Germans, finding these apparently abandoned stockpiles, believed that British morale was broken and that the BEF was in headlong flight (Terraine 1972: 151). This mistaken belief led General Alexander von Kluck to accede to Generaloberst Karl von Bülow's request for support in attacking the French V Armée, a decision that exposed the right flank of Kluck's 1. Armee to the decisive counter-attack by the unbroken BEF and VI Armée that opened the battle of the Marne on 6 September 1914 and changed the course of the war.

In fact, during the retreat from Mons, morale in the BEF would generally remain high, with one or two exceptions. Unaware of the strategic picture that made the British retreat inevitable, the men of the BEF had no idea why they were withdrawing. Those who had been in combat felt that they had given a good account of themselves and, man for man, were more than a match for the enemy. On 6 September, all ranks were pleased to end the weary retreat;

EN GUERRE = Hussards Anglais allant au front.

morale soared, and, in some units, a spontaneous cheer went up as the men learned that they were to turn on their pursuers at last (Maurice 1921: 169).

One of the exceptions, however, occurred when General Sir Horace Smith-Dorrien's II Corps withdrew after the battle of Le Cateau. Many stragglers became separated from their units in the fighting and as the cavalry followed behind the infantry they constantly came upon individuals or small groups of men making their way southward. Where they could, the cavalry tried to point these men back to their units. On 27 August Major Tom Bridges was placed in command of two squadrons of the 4th Dragoon Guards to act as the rear-guard to cover the Allied troops withdrawing through Saint-Quentin. Two British infantry battalions stopped in the town and the exhausted, demoralized men refused to go any further. The two infantry COs, believing that they were cut off from the rest of the BEF, gave the town's mayor a promissory note that they would surrender to the advancing Germans rather than bring about the destruction of the town by fighting.

Bridges, thinking that there were no British troops left in Saint-Quentin, was shocked to discover more than 200 British stragglers in the town square, not to mention the two infantry battalions waiting to surrender. Bridges quickly recovered the promissory note and informed the two infantry COs that he would leave no British soldier alive in the town; by this threat he compelled them to resume their withdrawal southwards. Bridges bought a tin drum and penny whistle in a toy shop, gave the whistle to his squadron trumpeter, and the two of them set about rousing the dispirited stragglers by beating the drum and playing marching tunes on the whistle. Eventually, the men responded, some began to laugh and cheer, and Bridges shepherded them back onto the road and led them southwards until they were reunited with II Corps well after midnight (Bridges 1938: 86f).

It is noteworthy that the cavalrymen of the 4th Dragoon Guards maintained much higher morale than the infantrymen despite having taken part in the costly charge at Audregnies on 24 August, only three days before. In the British cavalry morale was consistently high as in each encounter with the German cavalry the British believed that they had got the upper hand. The only event to mar this self-confidence was the charge at Audregnies, but the dampening effect of this was quickly counter-acted by the combats at Cerizy–Moÿ and Néry (Coleman 1916: 51–52 & 78).

British hussars near Saint-Quentin, 1914. The NCO riding at the front of the column with his legs sticking forward gives an idea of why some described the British cavalry seat as 'grotesque'. (DEA/ BIBLIOTECA AMBROSIANA/ Getty Images)

Casteau

22 August 1914

BACKGROUND TO BATTLE

A German Modell 1894 enlisted men's cuirassier helmet. Not the 'lobster-tail' extension at the back, which made cuirassiers quite distinctive, even when the helmet was under its cloth cover in the field. (INTERFOTO/History/Alamy Stock Photo)

Friday 21 August was misty, making it difficult for the Royal Flying Corps to carry out reconnaissance flights, but the Cavalry Division's scouting patrols pushed north across the Mons–Condé Canal as soon as the various regiments had reached their respective brigade rendezvous points south-east of Mons. A few of these patrols sighted German cavalry patrols, but none made contact. The 4th Dragoon Guards pushed forward just over 4 miles (6.4km) from its overnight bivouac at Harmignies to Bois Là-Haut, some 2 miles (3.2km) south-east of Mons. Once there, A Sqn secured the Obourg Bridge over the Mons–Condé Canal while B Sqn and D Sqn prepared defensive positions north of Bois Là-Haut. After being relieved by 4th Bn, The Middlesex Regiment, the 4th Dragoon Guards (minus C Sqn) returned to the Cavalry Division rendezvous at Harmignies where the regiment remained until the next evening (Wright 1914). Major Tom Bridges, commanding C Sqn, had been ordered to take his squadron forward as 'contact squadron', i.e. to press on until the squadron definitely made contact with the Germans and to try to capture a few (Gibb 1925: 2). That afternoon C Sqn set off at about 1600hrs, probably crossing the Mons–Condé Canal at Nimy, and advanced north-east towards Saint-Denis. Bridges sent out scouting patrols that reported that the Germans were in great strength to the north, estimating that there were about 2,500 German cavalry at Soignies, 10 miles (16km) north-east of Mons, the BEF's concentration point. This was the 9. Kavallerie-Division from HKK 2, which bivouacked around Soignies that night.

In addition to the intelligence relayed to Bridges by his scouts, a retired Belgian Army officer told the British cavalrymen that he estimated about 450,000 Germans to be advancing south-westwards from Brussels (Bridges 1938: 76). This information indicated that there were very many more Germans advancing on the BEF than previously thought and, also, that the Germans were in great strength west of the BEF with the consequent possibility that they might envelop the BEF's left flank. This information was passed back to the Cavalry Division HQ, which in turn reported it to GHQ (General Headquarters). For some reason, Major-General Henry Wilson, General Staff Officer to Field Marshal Sir John French, dismissed these reports as exaggerated and it was only late the next day that GHQ began to appreciate the true scale and extent of the German advance.

On the evening of 21 August, C Sqn halted for the night at Saint-Denis, just north of the Mons–Condé Canal, but after dark Bridges moved the squadron away from the village, across the Mons–Brussels road, and into the shelter of a wooded slope just north of Maisières (Bridges 1938: 76). He put out pickets and kept the squadron on standby throughout the night with two troops saddled up and ready to deploy. The men rested with the reins tied to their wrists so that their horses could not stray. Some loosened the girths of their horses to allow them to breathe more freely, but the girths could be tightened in an instant if necessary. The squadron had been told that strict silence must be kept, so the men tied handkerchiefs to their horses' bits in order to muffle any jingling as the horses champed on the metal bars in their mouths (Clouting, cited in Van Emden 1996: 38–39).

The action at Casteau was the first time British troops had been in combat on the continent of Europe since the Crimean War, and it was almost 100 years since they had last fought in western Europe at Waterloo. It was, therefore, a very important combat from the British point of view and a number of individuals recorded their personal recollections of the affair to supplement the contemporary records in the regimental, brigade and divisional war diaries. From the German perspective, however, it was an insignificant skirmish between scouting patrols. It must be remembered that by 22 August the Germans had already been campaigning for 2½ weeks, had fought several large set-piece battles, and had suffered thousands of casualties. For the German cavalry in particular, after the heavy losses suffered by HKK 2 in the battle of Haelen, the daily skirmishes of reconnaissance patrols with the enemy were routine and 'small beer'. The action at Casteau, therefore, is merely mentioned in passing in the war diaries of Kürassier-Regiment 4 and the 13. Kavallerie-Brigade, the higher formation of which the regiment was a part, and is not mentioned at all in the records of the 9. Kavallerie-Division. To the best of my knowledge, the only personal recollection of the action by a German participant is the patrol report of Leutnant Graf Lothar von und zu Hoensbroech, recorded in the regimental history published after the war. This fact highlights one of the recurrent difficulties with researching small-unit actions in World War I: the paucity of accounts at the small-unit level from the German side, which must be kept in mind when reading the descriptions of the encounter actions between the British and German cavalry that follow.

The Pattern 1908 Cavalry Sword. Weighing 3lb 2oz (1.4kg) and with a blade length of 35in (89cm), this weapon remained the issue sword of the British cavalry until the arm was finally fully mechanized in 1941. A testimony to the excellence of its design is the fact that Lieutenant George Patton simply copied the Pattern 1908 Cavalry Sword when he 'designed' the Model 1913 Cavalry Saber for the US cavalry. (© Royal Armouries IX.2728)

1 1600hrs, 21 August: C Sqn 4th Dragoon Guards crosses the Mons–Condé Canal, probably at Nimy, as contact squadron for the Cavalry Division.

2 c.1700hrs, 21 August: C Sqn halts near Saint-Denis and sends out reconnaissance patrols to the north.

3 c.2200hrs, 21 August: C Sqn moves its position from Saint-Denis across the Mons–Brussels road to a more secure location north of Maisières.

4 0530hrs, 22 August: Leutnant Hoensbroech's *Zug* from Kürassier-Regiment 4 departs from the regimental bivouac near Soignies on a reconnaissance patrol towards Mons.

5 0600hrs, 22 August: C Sqn departs its overnight bivouac and moves north-east along the Mons–Brussels road. At c.0630hrs, the squadron halts at a farmstead on the Saint-Denis crossroads to water its horses.

6 c.0645hrs, 22 August: C Sqn sees Hoensbroech's *Zug* approaching and tries to ambush it. The German advanced scouts spot the British ambush, and the *Zug* turns back towards Casteau, hotly pursued by Captain Hornby and 1 and 4 Troops of C Sqn. Major Bridges follows behind with the other two troops.

7 c.0700hrs, 22 August: Hoensbroech's *Zug* is overtaken by Hornby's half-squadron and four German cuirassiers are captured, three being wounded. Hoensbroech is reinforced by a *Zug* from Ulanen-Regiment 13, which is on outpost duty at Casteau. In the ensuing mêlée several uhlans are killed or wounded. The British suffer no casualties.

8 c.0710hrs, 22 August: The German cavalry, both cuirassiers and uhlans, withdraws up the Mons–Brussels road towards Soignies. They are joined by Leutnant Humann's *Zug* from Husaren-Regiment 8, the entire combined force still being pursued by Hornby's half-squadron.

9 c.0720hrs, 22 August: Bicycle-mounted German troops, as part of the 9. Kavallerie-Division's vanguard, deploy into position on some high ground commanding the Mons–Brussels road to give fire support to the retreating German cavalrymen.

10 c.0730hrs, 22 August: On coming under fire from the cyclists, Hornby dismounts his 1 and 4 Troops under cover of the walled garden of the Château de Casteau and returns fire. Corporal Thomas shoots a German officer at a range of 400yd (366m). The remainder of C Sqn reinforces Hornby.

11 c.0745hrs, 22 August: C Sqn withdraws unmolested to Obourg, crosses the Mons–Condé Canal, and later re-joins the 4th Dragoon Guards at Harmignies.

Battlefield environment

The action at Casteau was in an area bounded on the south by the Mons–Condé Canal. North of the canal the ground rose steeply to a ridge and then dropped slightly into undulating terrain until north of Soignies it became quite broken with steep-sided hills. The Mons–Brussels road, along which all of the action took place, fell away from the high ground around Maisières down to Casteau, which lay in the shallow valley adjacent to the Aubrecheuil stream, to rise again as the road ascended the long incline towards Soignies. The road was lined with poplar trees and was 30ft (9m) wide, with a *pavé* surface and a tramline running down one side (Gibb 1925: 3). The countryside through which the road passed was a mixture of arable fields and woodland. By late August the corn in the fields had been harvested and the sheaves gathered into stooks, but as most of the men had been called up for military service, the stooks had not yet been cleared for threshing and nor had the hay been built into haystacks.

Owing to the clear early-morning light and the long gradual slopes along which the road ran, visibility was good apart from where buildings obstructed the view. From Casteau the Aubrecheuil flowed almost due south towards the Mons–Condé Canal through a wooded and steep-sided valley in which lay the village of Saint-Denis. This valley provided good cover for the rendezvous point from which C Sqn 4th Dragoon Guards could send out scouting patrols. It would have provided a suitably covert place to bivouac for the night. Major Bridges, however, suspected a number of men, who pedalled off on bicycles northwards out of Saint-Denis soon after the squadron arrived, of being German soldiers in civilian clothing. After dark, therefore, he moved the squadron westward away from the village, across the Mons–Brussels road, and into cover on the wooded northern slope of the ridge near to Maisières, which he had noted earlier as the squadron deployed north of the Mons–Condé Canal (Bridges 1938: 76).

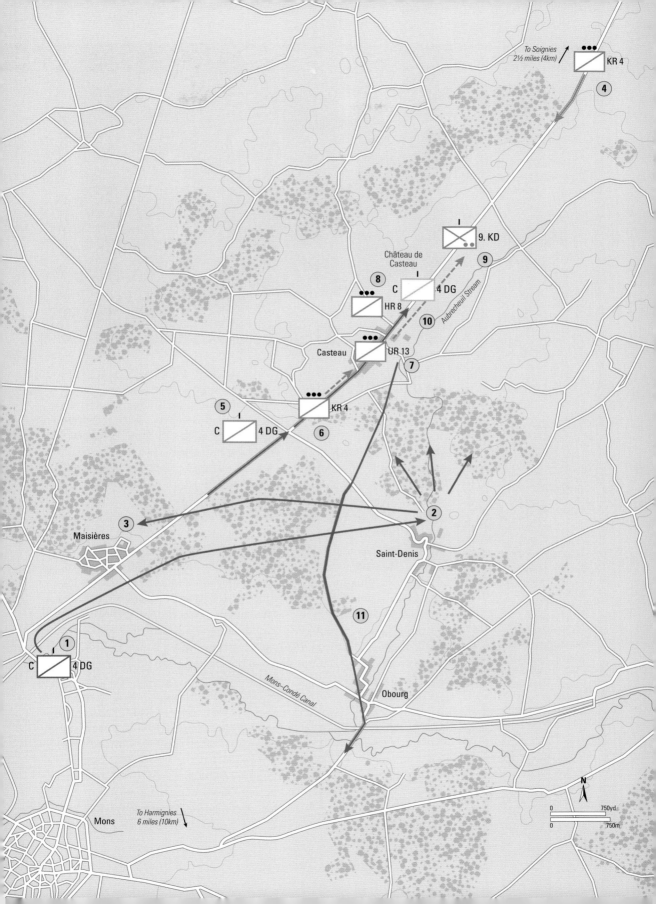

To Soignies
2½ miles (4km)

KR 4

④

9. KD

Château de
Casteau

⑨

C   4 DG

⑧

HR 8

Aubrecheuil Stream

Casteau

UR 13

⑩

⑦

⑤

KR 4

C   4 DG

⑥

②

Maisières

Saint-Denis

③

⑪

①

C   4 DG

Mons–Condé Canal

Obourg

Mons

To Harmignies
6 miles (10km)

N

0   750yd
0   750m

British cavalry during the retreat from Mons, August 1914. Note the French interpreter (third figure from the left) talking to the British troop commander (leftmost figure). Each British Army cavalry regiment had a French interpreter attached to it when it arrived in France. (Daily Mirror/Mirrorpix/Mirrorpix via Getty Images)

OPPOSITE

The German Modell 1890 *Stahlrohrlanze* weighed 4lb 11oz (2.1kg) and was 10ft 3½in (3.1m) long, 5in (12.7cm) of which was the blade. The German cavalryman was trained to use the lance at the couch because it was long and heavy, which affected its balance and made it difficult to handle unless firmly seated under the armpit (Pelet-Narbonne 1911: 205*f*). In addition, it was found that, without the impetus of a galloping horse behind it, the steel blade did not readily penetrate clothing. In a mêlée, therefore, the lance proved unwieldy and ineffective, which disadvantaged the Germans in mounted combat against foes armed with the sword or a lighter, handier lance. (© Royal Armouries VII.1647)

INTO COMBAT

The night of 21/22 August passed uneventfully for Bridges' C Sqn and at about 0600hrs he decided to push the squadron north-eastwards along the Mons–Brussels road towards Soignies until he found some Germans. The road, which was lined with poplar trees, was very wide, being some 30ft (9m) across, and was paved with large square flagstones, with a tramline running down one side (Gibb 1925: 3). The smooth *pavé* surface of the road was slippery for horses shod with metal horseshoes.

Just over 1 mile (1.6km) south-west of Casteau, at about 0630hrs the squadron halted at a farmstead on the Saint-Denis crossroads to water its horses when reports came in that a German reconnaissance patrol was approaching down the road from Casteau (Bridges 1938: 76). The German patrol was from Kürassier-Regiment 4, and was commanded by Hoensbroech, who was nonchalantly smoking a cigar as he led his men down the road (Thomas 1938: 41). Bridges, realizing that his squadron was out of sight behind some farm buildings at the crossroads, and anticipating that the German patrol would continue down the road, quickly conceived a plan to try to capture it. He ordered 2 and 3 Troops to dismount and wait in ambush while 1 and 4 Troops were to remain mounted with swords drawn, ready to pursue if necessary. For all his nonchalance, clearly Hoensbroech was alert, and when the advanced scouts of the German patrol were about 300yd (274m) from the ambush, a British soldier's incautious movement gave the game away, causing the German scouts to halt and then turn back towards Casteau (Bridges 1938: 76–77).

Captain Charles Hornby, second-in-command of C Sqn, immediately requested permission to pursue the withdrawing German patrol with 1 and 4 Troops and, on getting it, set off at a gallop after the Germans while Bridges mounted 2 and 3 Troops and followed at a trot. Seeing half a squadron of

British cavalry in pursuit, the Germans too spurred their horses to a gallop in an endeavour to escape. The Germans' horses, however, were already somewhat jaded from 18 days' campaigning while the British horses, having just arrived in theatre, were still fresh and in good condition (Hoensbroech, cited in Glasmeier 1932: 55; Worrell, cited in Ascoli 2001: 52). The width of the Mons–Brussels road allowed the British to adopt squadron-column formation, with 1 and 4 Troops in line abreast one behind the other. Ben Gunn, an Englishman who lived near Casteau, cheered on the British cavalrymen as they galloped past his home (Ascoli 2001: 53; Gibb 1925: 4; Van Emden 1996: 46). One or two horses stumbled and fell on the slippery *pavé* road surface (Bulmer, cited in Anglesey 1996: 113). The road surface, however, hindered the tired German mounts more than the British and, so, after a 1-mile (1.6km) chase, on the outskirts of Casteau, Hornby and his men caught up with the German patrol. In the ensuing mêlée four of the German cuirassiers were captured by the British, three of them wounded. The fourth, Gefreiter Schuer, later managed to escape and made his way back to Kürassier-Regiment 4 that night (Glasmeier 1932: 55).

Hoensbroech's *Zug* (platoon), however, had retreated onto a mounted *Zug* from Ulanen-Regiment 13, which was on outpost duty at the southern entrance to Casteau, where the wide Mons–Brussels road narrowed as it passed through the town. Hornby, with 1 Troop in the lead, charged down the main street straight into the German uhlan formation, the pursuit of the cuirassiers and the assault on the uhlans becoming, in effect, one single mêlée. A number of the uhlans were killed or wounded in the initial onslaught. Once the British had charged into the uhlans, however, and the impetus of their charge was broken, they had to engage in hand-to-hand fighting with the Germans and, thus, lost the advantage of longer reach with their swords which they had in the charge. The uhlans were unable to manoeuvre, however, hemmed in as they were by the houses lining the street, and were also in some confusion, being disordered by the fleeing cuirassiers seconds before the British dragoons smashed into them. In the confined space of the street the Germans were unable to wield their lances effectively. Several threw down their lances and resorted to their swords during the mêlée. The noise was tremendous, with horse hooves clattering on the stones of the *pavé* road and men shouting (Worrell, cited in Ascoli 2001: 53). At the same time, Belgian armed civilians started firing on the German cavalrymen from the houses on either side of the street, causing further confusion (Gibb 1925: 4; Glasmeier 1932: 55).

In the initial onslaught Hornby ran one uhlan through as he and 1 Troop charged into the German line, knocking the uhlan out of his saddle. Warrant Officer Class 2 Sharpe, the squadron sergeant major, also struck down an uhlan. Sergeant Barrett ran his sword straight through a German until his thumb was pressed against the man's chest. Private Tilney, Hornby's orderly, sparred with a German, but neither could strike the other, the duel ending when the German surrendered to Tilney. Private Bulmer stabbed another German in his left arm, at which his adversary turned his horse and fled (Anglesey 1996: 113; Ascoli 2001: 53; Van Emden 1996: 40; Vaughan 1954: 163). In a very short time, the German cuirassiers and uhlans were rapidly retreating through Casteau and up the wide road back towards Soignies.

British lancers riding ahead of their regiment as advanced scouts in Belgium, 1914. Clearly visible are the leather loops through which the right arm was inserted to help support the lance when it was at rest in the lance-bucket attached to the right stirrup. The men are wearing their greatcoats due to the cold winter weather. As these men are apparently not part of a squadron formation, they are probably advanced scouts of their regiment. British cavalry doctrine, however, stated that when a pair of advanced scouts was advancing towards the enemy, one scout should have his rifle in his hands, ready to use, and the other should be holding his drawn sword or lance. As neither of these men has a weapon at the ready, they are probably somewhere behind the front line and, therefore, not expecting to meet the enemy. They are, perhaps, riding ahead of their regiment to mark out billets or a bivouac for the night. (Robert Hunt Library/Windmill Books/ UIG via Getty Images)

They were joined by Leutnant Rolf von Humann's *Zug* from Husaren-Regiment 8, which had come in from a side road in support. Under pressure of 1 Troop's charge, the German hussars, too, were compelled to withdraw (Bridges 1938: 77; Westecker 1939: 110). Indeed, the soldiers of 1 Troop 4th Dragoon Guards had charged with such impetus and aggression that, by the time 4 Troop under Lieutenant Swallow caught up with them in Casteau, the mêlée was over, and the Germans were hastily retreating towards Soignies, hotly pursued by Hornby (Clouting, cited in Van Emden 1996: 40).

The Germans continued retreating up the road towards Soignies well knowing that the vanguard of the 9. Kavallerie-Division was not far away. It was, in fact, only about 1 mile (1.6km) from the northern edge of Casteau and consisted of bicycle-mounted troops. These cyclists were either the *Radfahr-Compagnie* of one of the *Jäger* battalions or cavalrymen who had been mounted on bicycles due to losses of horses during the advance across Belgium. On 22 August, no *Jäger* battalion was attached to the 9. Kavallerie-Division, all of them being assigned to the other two divisions in HKK 2 (Poseck 1921: 35), so it seems likely that the cyclists were cavalrymen rather than *Jäger*. In either case, when they saw the harried group of cuirassiers, uhlans and hussars retreating up the long slope towards them, still pursued by Hornby's half-squadron of dragoons, the cyclists deployed on either side of the road to provide covering fire for their compatriots.

By this time the horses in Hornby's command were blown and, seeing the German cyclists deploying into firing positions on the hill crest about 400yd (366m) away, he ordered 1 and 4 Troops to dismount and return fire. The British dragoons had reached the grounds of the Château de Casteau on the

German uhlans advancing. Note the distinctive *Tschapka* headgear that marked uhlans out as traditional lancers, even though all German cavalry regiments were issued with the lance from 1890. Uhlans also wore the distinctive double-breasted *ulanka* field-service jacket. Hussars, on the other hand, wore a busby and the equally distinctive *attila* field-service jacket with its rows of embroidered button loops across the breast. So, even though the German cavalry deployed in field-grey service uniform and were all armed with the lance, it was still possible for the informed to distinguish between uhlans, hussars, cuirassiers and dragoons.(SOTK2011/Alamy Stock Photo)

western side of the road, the walled grounds of which offered cover from the German rifle-fire for the led horses. The horse-holders, therefore, quickly took 1 and 4 Troops' horses into this cover. At this point, coming under enemy fire for the first time, 4 Troop's commander, Swallow, fell to pieces and was unable to master himself. In disgust Hornby ordered Swallow to get under cover with the led horses (Van Emden 1996: 42). As the men of 4 Troop dismounted, Corporal Ernest Thomas quickly grabbed his rifle out of its bucket and, seeing a German officer directing the cyclists into position, took aim and fired the first shot taken in anger by a British soldier in Europe in 59 years. The range was about 400yd (366m), but it was a good shot and the German officer fell from his horse, either wounded or killed (Thomas 1939: 41).

Bridges joined Hornby with 2 and 3 Troops, and these dismounted to give covering fire to 1 and 4 Troops, allowing them to retire before the superior force of Germans now massing on the road. They retired through Casteau,

German *Jäger* in Brussels, 1914. Each *Höherer Kavallerie-Kommandeur* had a number of *Jäger* battalions attached to it to provide more firepower to the under-gunned cavalry regiments. As light infantry, the *Jäger* and *Schutzen* wore distinctive uniforms, including the *Tschako* (pictured here) instead of the *Pickelhaube*, and a green uniform rather than the standard field-grey of the rest of the German Army. The *Jäger* or *Schutzen* battalions considered themselves élite infantry, a status confirmed by the fact that, unlike standard infantry battalions, each *Jäger* battalion had an integral machine-gun detachment, a bicycle company and motor-lorry transport. (INTERFOTO/Alamy Stock Photo)

A dramatic depiction of the first encounter between British and German cavalry at Casteau, taken from the *Penny War Weekly, Vol. 1 No. 2*, 12 September 1914. The artist has managed to capture the scene remarkably well and accurately. The written description of the encounter, however, contains several errors including incorrectly identifying the British cavalry as hussars and the town as being in France instead of Belgium. As World War I progressed the illustrations and accounts in the popular press became ever more lurid and less accurate as the press willingly promoted and believed jingoistic propaganda. (Chronicle/Alamy Stock Photo)

requisitioning some carts from Mr Gunn into which they put their prisoners and the discarded German lances scattered on the main street of the town (Gibb 1925: 4). Bridges sent a message to the 2nd Cavalry Brigade suggesting that, if he were reinforced, it might be possible to deliver a flanking attack on the German left wing and stop the advance of the 9. Kavallerie-Division, but he was ordered to re-join the 4th Dragoon Guards at Harmignies (Bridges 1939: 77). This was because GHQ had finally begun to appreciate the threat of a German envelopment on the open western flank of the BEF and had ordered the Cavalry Division to cross from east to west in the rear of the infantry moving up to Mons in order to occupy a position on the BEF's left wing. This night march along slippery *pavé* roads, crossing columns of marching infantry, was exhausting for both men and horses (Home & Briscoe 1985: 16–17). Many of the cavalry regiments only reached their designated assembly points in the early hours of 23 August. For example, the 4th Dragoon Guards, setting off from Harmignies at 2030hrs on 22 August, only arrived at the regimental assembly point at 0300hrs on 23 August (Wright 1914).

The British casualties in this encounter at Casteau were one man lightly wounded plus two horses killed and three wounded. The British accounts, while varying slightly in detail, generally agree that between four and eight Germans were taken prisoner, and eight to ten uhlans were killed in the mêlée. Recently, however, two British military historians have raised doubts over these claims, despite the unanimous agreement of all the British eyewitness accounts (Cooksey & Murland 2014: 39). They do so on the basis that the British accounts invariably refer to the German cavalry as uhlans, whereas in fact they were cuirassiers, and that the regimental history of Kürassier-Regiment 4 specifically states that the regiment suffered no casualties in the action, other than the four cuirassiers taken prisoner. This, however, ignores the fact that three different German cavalry regiments took part in the action. While historians can refer to both the war diary and the published regimental history of Kürassier-Regiment 4, they cannot do so for Husaren-Regiment 8 and Ulanen-Regiment 13 as the German records are unfortunately incomplete. I have been unable to find any trace of published regimental histories for these last two regiments in the catalogue of the *Deutsche Nationalbibliothek*. They appear never to have been published before their respective war diaries were destroyed in the bombing of Potsdam in 1944. We cannot know, therefore, what casualties were suffered by the hussar and uhlan units in the encounter. Furthermore, the claim that none of the British eyewitnesses was able to distinguish between German cuirassiers, uhlans and hussars, when these three types of cavalry wore different and, in the case of uhlans and hussars, very distinctive uniforms, is certainly untrue. In fact, Bridges was an expert on the German cavalry, having visited them before the war and having translated General der Kavallerie Bernhardi's influential book, *Cavalry in War and Peace*, from the original German. When Bridges says, therefore, that 'uhlans' were killed and that 'hussars' were pursued by Hornby, it is safe to assume that he knew what he was talking about. For these reasons, therefore, I would refute the doubts expressed by Cooksey and Murland and assume that the number of German casualties given in the British eyewitness accounts is roughly correct and that the fatalities were indeed uhlans from Ulanen-Regiment 13.

British Army medical personnel from a field ambulance carry a stretchered casualty to a horse-drawn ambulance, 1914. Ambulances such as these were used to recover the wounded of both sides after the action at Cerizy. German complaints that the British provided inadequate medical treatment to their wounded are rather unfair. A field ambulance was not equipped to provide advanced medical care to the wounded, but simply to provide basic initial care where possible and then to move the wounded back to a field hospital for proper treatment. (Henry Guttmann Collection/Hulton Archive/ Getty Images)

Cerizy–Moÿ

28 August 1914

BACKGROUND TO BATTLE

Saturday 22 August saw a number of skirmishes between the German and British cavalry as General Alexander von Kluck's 1. Armee continued its advance through Belgium. These patrol encounters were the first inkling the German High Command had that the BEF had arrived on the Continent.

Next day, the 1. Armee ran into the main force of the BEF, which had assembled at Mons in compliance with the request of Général Joseph Joffre, Commander-in-Chief of French forces on the Western Front, that the British align themselves on the western flank of Général de Division Charles Lanrezac's V Armée. Both sides were surprised by the encounter. To the British the intensity, range and accuracy of the German artillery fire came as a surprise, as did the relentlessness of the German attack. The Germans were equally surprised by the steadfastness of the British soldiers in defence and their rapid and accurate rifle fire. Nevertheless, by the end of the day the BEF had been driven back 3 miles (4.8km) by the Germans, who were attacking in overwhelming numbers. That night Field Marshal Sir John French learned that Lanrezac's V Armée had retreated after heavy fighting in the Sambre valley, thus exposing the BEF's right flank. Consequently, French ordered the BEF to withdraw southwards to try to conform with the rapidly retreating V Armée.

The BEF, however, was unable to break contact with the pursuing Germans on 24 and 25 August. Instead, a series of small rear-guard actions merely allowed the British to hold the Germans at arm's length. The most notable of these, from a cavalry perspective, was the action at Audregnies on the morning of 24 August. On the evening of 25 August, General Sir Horace Smith-Dorrien, GOC (General Officer Commanding) II Corps, realized that he had to stop the

These German dragoons, marching in file during manoeuvres, wear peacetime uniforms. On the outbreak of World War I, the field-grey service uniform was issued, and the colourful barrack dress put in store. They carry their lances slung by a loop over the shoulder and with the butt-spike in the lance bucket attached to the stirrup. The lances have their pennons unfurled. (ullstein bild/ullstein bild via Getty Images)

pursuing Germans in their tracks in order to give his weary troops the chance to break contact, reorganize and rest. As his troops straggled into bivouacs around Le Cateau, he decided to stand and fight. He asked Major-General Sir Edmund Allenby for the support of the Cavalry Division, which was quickly confirmed. He also asked Général Jean-François Sordet, who had assembled his Corps du Cavalerie to the west of the BEF, for assistance. French agreed to Smith-Dorrien's plan but, inexplicably, he allowed Lieutenant-General Sir Douglas Haig's I Corps to continue its withdrawal southwards, leaving II Corps and the Cavalry Division to face the Germans on their own on 26 August. Inevitably, Kluck's immensely more powerful 1. Armee outflanked II Corps on both wings and threatened to encircle it, thus forcing it to abandon its positions and carry out a difficult daylight fighting withdrawal. Nevertheless, the British had put up such stiff resistance that II Corps was allowed to retire unmolested and, thanks also to the timely attacks by Sordet's Corps du Cavalerie on the western flank of the 1. Armee, II Corps finally managed to break contact with Kluck's troops on the night of 26/27 August.

The BEF continued its withdrawal southwards, trying to keep aligned with Lanrezac's V Armée, which was pulling back across the Oise River. Haig's I Corps retired via Landrecies down the eastern side of the Forêt de Mormal, while the columns of Smith-Dorrien's II Corps retreated down the western side of the forest, creating a gap of some 15 miles (24km) between the two halves of the BEF. By chance Generalleutnant Freiherr Manfred von Richthofen's HKK 1 (the Garde-Kavallerie-Division and the

British lancers water their horses in a French river, 1914. The knowledge of how to water, feed and exercise the horses correctly was a fundamental part of horsemastership, as getting it wrong could give the horses colic, thus rendering them unfit for service. (Daily Mirror/Mirrorpix/Mirrorpix via Getty Images)

5. Kavallerie-Division) advanced into this gap. Attached to I Corps was the 5th (Independent) Cavalry Brigade under Brigadier-General Sir Philip Chetwode. This brigade consisted of the 2nd Dragoons (The Royal Scots Greys), the 12th (Prince of Wales's Royal) Lancers, the 20th Hussars and J Bty RHA (Royal Horse Artillery). Brigadier-General Hubert Gough's 3rd Cavalry Brigade also attached itself to Haig's I Corps, deliberately separating itself from the Cavalry Division, which it made no effort to re-join, reflecting the unwarranted disdain in which Gough held Allenby. These two cavalry brigades covered I Corps, while the rest of the Cavalry Division (the 1st, 2nd and 4th Cavalry brigades) provided a protective screen to cover the battered II Corps as it withdrew. After the war, the semi-official history of the German cavalry campaign in Belgium and France acknowledged that the British cavalry performed this difficult task admirably (Poseck 1921: 73).

On 28 August I Corps continued its southerly withdrawal from Guise towards La Fère. As the location of II Corps and the Cavalry Division was not known to Haig, he created a flank guard to cover his I Corps to the west. This flank guard, under the command of Brigadier-General Henry Horne RFA (Royal Field Artillery), consisted of the 5th Infantry Brigade and the 5th (Independent) Cavalry Brigade. Horne ordered the infantry to move southwards down the eastern bank of the Oise and the 5th Cavalry Brigade to move down the western bank. The 5th Cavalry Brigade was ordered to rendezvous at 0600hrs at Le Mont, a hill about ½ mile (0.8km) south-west of Thenelles and about 9 miles (14.5km) east of Saint-Quentin. Here the Army Service Corps performed wonders in replenishing the brigade's supplies of rations for both men and horses. The 12th Lancers sent reconnaissance patrols westwards towards Mesnil-Saint-Laurent and Neuville-Saint-Amand, but found no sign of the advancing Germans. By 1100hrs the infantry had made such good progress that the 5th Cavalry Brigade had effectively become the rear guard of I Corps (Howard-Vyse 1921). Chetwode located his brigade headquarters at La Guignette Farm on a crossroads on the RN 44, the main road running between Saint-Quentin and La Fère, some 6 miles (10km) south of Saint-Quentin.

British cavalry marching through a French town. The cavalry on both sides frequently found themselves marching and counter-marching long distances as the staff officers at GHQ directed them to move from one flank of the army to the other, often countermanding orders issued only a few hours previously. This was particularly wearing on both horses and men and, in the case of the German cavalry, certainly hindered their ability to pursue the BEF after Mons. (Author's Collection)

In the hamlet of Cerizy, about 500yd (457m) west of La Guignette, were B Sqn and C Sqn 20th Hussars, A Sqn having been detached to assist the 5th Infantry Brigade to the east of the Oise. The 20th Hussars sent out reconnaissance patrols towards Urvillers and Essigny-le-Grand, which reported all clear. About 1¼ miles (2km) east-south-east of Brigade HQ was the town of Moÿ-de-l'Aisne, where the men of the 12th Lancers were resting in the grounds of the local château, as the regiment had been appointed brigade reserve once it had completed its earlier reconnaissance missions. In some dead ground halfway between La Guignette and Moÿ, the Scots Greys and J Bty RHA were in position. The Scots Greys had been ordered to provide the day outposts, with one troop under Lieutenant Callander occupying Point 114, a tactically important hill some ¾ mile (1.2km) to the north of La Guignette, which dominated the RN 44 as well as La Folie and Puisieux farms.

Richthofen's HKK 1 was ordered to bypass Saint-Quentin round the east and to interdict the roads leading south in order to cut off any Allied troops remaining in the vicinity of the town. The major road the German cavalry were to block was the RN 44 leading to La Fère. Generalmajor Günther von Etzel's Garde-Kavallerie-Division started the day near Wassigny and advanced on Itancourt, with the Garde-Jäger-Bataillon's Cyclist Company (Hauptmann von Kretschmann) brushing aside French resistance at Homblières about 4 miles (6.4km) due east of Saint-Quentin. Generalmajor Karl von Ilsemann's 5. Kavallerie-Division, however, was held up by strong French defensive positions at Thenelles. Consequently, the Garde-Kavallerie-Division pushed on past Saint-Quentin alone to carry out HKK 1's mission. The 1. Garde-Kavallerie-Brigade (the Garde du Corps regiment and the 2. Garde-Kürassier-Regiment) covered the German western flank facing Saint-Quentin, while Oberst Freiherr von Senden's 3. Garde-Kavallerie-Brigade (the 1. and 2. Garde-Dragoner-Regimenter) became the division's vanguard pressing on to cut the RN 44 south of Saint-Quentin (Poseck 1921: 73). The 2. Garde-Kavallerie-Brigade, which consisted of two regiments of *Garde-Ulanen*, was divisional reserve.

MAP KEY

1 1100hrs: The 5th (Independent) Cavalry Brigade is in position between Moÿ-de-l'Aisne and Cerizy as rear-guard to I Corps BEF.

2 1330hrs: Patrols of the 3. Garde-Kavallerie-Brigade, the advanced guard of HKK 1, are first seen by British outposts.

3 1600hrs: Lieutenant Callander's troop from C Sqn Scots Greys is driven from Point 114 by 1./1. GDR.

4 1620hrs: Three squadrons of the 1. and 2. Garde-Dragoner-Regimenter gallop into the Vallée de l'Hôtellerie with the intention of launching a mounted attack on the British defensive line on the opposite slope.

5 1630hrs: C Sqn Scots Greys opens fire on the advancing Germans.

6 c.1630hrs: C Sqn 12th Lancers and the regiment's machine-gun section dismount on Point 109 and open fire on the advancing Germans.

7 c.1640hrs: 3 Sec J Bty RHA gallops into action and opens fire on the advancing Germans.

8 c.1645hrs: A Sqn and B Sqn 12th Lancers are ordered to move via dead ground into a position from which to enfilade the eastern flank of the reserve squadrons of the 2. Garde-Dragoner-Regiment near Puisieux Farm.

9 c.1650hrs: 1. and 4./1. GDR are ordered to withdraw from their exposed positions back to their led horses near La Folie Farm. This order does not reach Leutnant Graf von Schwerin and his *Zug* from 4./1. GDR.

10 c.1700hrs: C Sqn 12th Lancers charges and overruns Schwerin's *Zug*. When the lancers attack, 1 Sec and 3 Sec J Bty RHA lift their fire and hit the Garde-Schützen-Bataillon assembly area in the wood north of La Folie Farm.

11 c.1700hrs: C Sqn 20th Hussars advances two troops dismounted to Point 116 and one troop mounted to attack the Germans around Lambay Farm. The mounted attack is called off.

12 c.1715hrs: A Sqn and B Sqn Scots Greys join the 12th Lancers on the German position.

13 c.1715hrs: B Sqn 20th Hussars advances north along the axis of the RN 44 until forced to retire by fire from Batterie Graf Roedern.

14 c.1730hrs: The Germans shell the road while the 20th Hussars withdraws to Cerizy via a covered route in dead ground.

15 c.1745hrs: The 3. Garde-Kavallerie-Brigade falls back 1 mile (1.6km) to the north to the ridgeline held by the uhlans of the 2. Garde-Kavallerie-Brigade.

Battlefield environment

Friday 28 August was another hot autumnal day. The day started cool and misty, presaging the high temperatures of later in the day. The eyewitness accounts state that by midday the heat was 'scorching'. The terrain was hilly and undulating, with several hidden valleys and much dead ground, which allowed forces to manoeuvre unseen. This fact was used to good effect by the British to mask their initial dispositions as well as in both the charge by the 12th Lancers and the withdrawal of the 20th Hussars, but the Germans do not seem to have tried to exploit the possibilities for covered movement provided by the terrain. The area of the battle was a farming district and the slopes of most of the hills and valleys were covered with fields of arable crops. The corn had already been harvested and the sheaves had been loosely piled into stooks, which crossed the fields in irregular lines in preparation for being gathered and stacked in haystacks. The valley bottoms were planted with a root crop, probably beets. Nevertheless, the fields provided cover neither from view nor from fire. Here and there were walled farmsteads – La Guignette, La Folie, Puisieux and Lambay – which, because they were defensible against small-arms fire, made convenient assembly points for troops and led horses and sites for regimental and brigade headquarters.

The general area of combat on 28 August was within a box marked by the towns of Urvillers, Berthenicourt, Benay and Moÿ-de-l'Aisne at the four corners. The area was bounded on the east by the Oise River running north–south between Berthenicourt and Moÿ with the small town of Alaincourt lying between them, all three on the west bank of the Oise. The only other settlement was the hamlet of Cerizy, lying between Benay and Moÿ. The area was bisected by the RN 44, the main road running between Saint-Quentin and La Fère, which the 5th Cavalry Brigade was overwatching and which the Garde-Kavallerie-Division had been ordered to interdict in order to cut off any Allied troops remaining in Saint-Quentin.

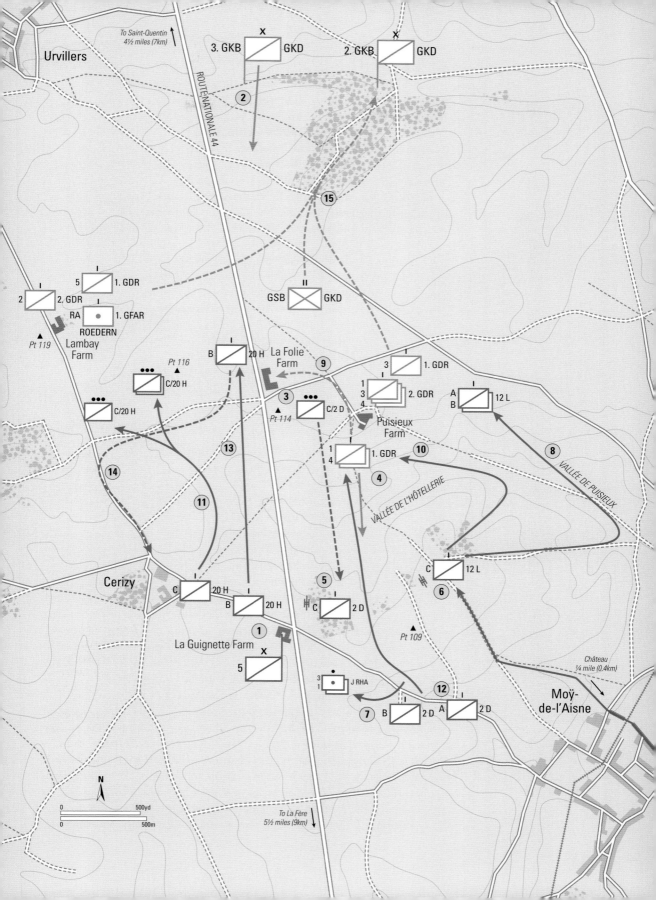

To Saint-Quentin
4½ miles (7km)

Urvillers

ROUTE NATIONALE 44

3. GKB ⊠ **GKD**

②

2. GKB ⊠ **GKD**

⑮

5 1. GDR

2 2. GDR

RA ● 1. GFAR
ROEDERN

▲ Pt 119
Lambay Farm

GSB ⊠ **GKD**

●●● C/20 H

▲ Pt 116

●●● C/20 H

B 20 H

La Folie Farm

⑨

3 1. GDR

1 3 4 2. GDR

A B 12 L

③
▲ Pt 114

●●● C/2 D

Puisieux Farm

⑬

1 4 1. GDR

⑩

⑧

VALLÉE DE PUISIEUX

⑭

⑪

VALLÉE DE L'HÔTELLERIE

Cerizy

C 20 H

B 20 H

⑤

C 2 D

▲ Pt 109

C 12 L

⑥

①

La Guignette Farm

5 ⊠

3 1 ● J RHA

⑫

Château
¼ mile (0.4km)

Moÿ-
de-l'Aisne

⑦

B 2 D

A 2 D

N

0 ———— 500yd
0 ———— 500m

To La Fère
5½ miles (9km)

INTO COMBAT

Around 1330hrs, British outposts of the 5th Cavalry Brigade reported German cavalry advancing southwards from Itancourt towards the RN 44. There was some desultory skirmishing, but to the bemusement of the British the Germans did not press forward vigorously. This was because the French 10ᵉ Bataillon Territorial had attacked from Saint-Quentin threatening the right flank of the 3. Garde-Kavallerie-Brigade. The French attack was repulsed by the 1. Garde-Kavallerie-Brigade and the Garde-Jäger-Bataillon during the afternoon. The Garde-Schützen-Bataillon moved up to support the 3. Garde-Kavallerie-Brigade. The Germans knew that there was British cavalry at Cerizy, but were not aware that there was more British cavalry around Moÿ.

At 1600hrs Senden, believing the British cavalry outposts to be no more than weak and shattered enemy forces, decided to attack them with three mounted squadrons supported by the remaining squadrons dismounted (Vogel 1916: 55). Two of the dismounted squadrons, 2./2. GDR and 5./1. GDR, supported by the six 7.7cm field guns of Batterie Graf Roedern from the *Reiter-Abteilung* ('mounted detachment') of the 1. Garde-Feldartillerie-Regiment, were sent south of Urvillers to cover the western flank of the 3. Garde-Kavallerie-Brigade. The eastern flank, facing Alaincourt, was covered by 1. and 3./2. GDR and 3./1. GDR (Geßler 1927: 23). The lead mounted squadron was Rittmeister von Rheinbaben's 1./1. GDR, followed by Rittmeister Graf von Hohenthal's 4./1. GDR. Behind them was Rittmeister von Levetzow's 4./2. GDR.

As the Germans advanced, Callander's troop from C Sqn Scots Greys, which had occupied Point 114 with its horses under cover on the reverse side of the hill, opened fire on 1./1. GDR. The Germans, too, dismounted and skirmished forward, forcing the Scots Greys soldiers to withdraw back to the main body of their regiment across the Vallée de l'Hôtellerie. This was a steep-sided valley lying between Points 114 and 109, running south-east–north-west and about 1,200yd (1.1km) wide. Its slopes were bare, consisting of harvested fields of corn, the sheaves of which had been gathered in lines of stooks, while the fields at the bottom of the valley had been planted with a root crop. Having secured La Folie and Puisieux farms, Rheinbaben's 1./1. GDR had remounted, and the three German squadrons galloped over the northern lip of the Vallée de l'Hôtellerie in column of troops formation. Across the valley, C Sqn Scots Greys, under Major Foster Swetenham, had been deployed in a defensive position that overlooked the RN 44 and the Vallée de l'Hôtellerie across which the Germans would have to advance once they had secured La Folie and Puisieux farms. With C Sqn were the Maxim guns of the Scots Greys' machine-gun section, commanded by Lieutenant George Pigot-Moodie. The British immediately opened rapid fire on the advancing German dragoons.

At Moÿ the personnel of the 12th Lancers were taking advantage of the opportunity of being brigade reserve to do some necessary maintenance of equipment and for the men to have a wash and a shave in the lake in the grounds of the local château. The horses were off-saddled, watered and allowed to graze. The machine-gun section under Lieutenant William Styles was overhauling its Maxim guns and pack-saddlery. Some men were sleeping on the grass or writing letters home. At about 1610hrs, hearing rifle fire coming from the north-west, Lieutenant-Colonel Frank Wormald, the CO, ordered the regiment to follow-on while he went forward with the regimental headquarters to find out what was happening. In a very short space of time, C Sqn had saddled-up, mounted and followed Wormald. Many of the men had not had time to pull on their field jackets or caps and mounted-up in their shirtsleeves. The squadron was commanded by Captain John Michell because the squadron commander, Major Percy Bailey, had accidentally shot himself and had been captured by the Germans while in hospital. Following immediately behind C Sqn was the machine-gun section, but A Sqn and B Sqn took a little longer to saddle-up. At about 1630hrs when C Sqn and the 12th Lancers' machine-gun section joined Wormald on the north-eastern side of Point 109, he ordered the men to dismount, form a firing line and immediately engage the three German squadrons, which were now visible some 1,000yd (914m) distant galloping down the opposite slope into the Vallée de l'Hôtellerie. The C Sqn horses were led under cover on the reverse slope of the hill while the men opened up a heavy rifle and machine-gun fire on the Germans.

About 5–10 minutes later the two quick-firing 13-pdr guns of No. 3 Section of J Bty RHA deployed for action to the rear of the two C Sqn firing lines at the head of a gully that gave a clear view into the Vallée de l'Hôtellerie, from whence they too opened fire over open sights at the advancing Germans in the valley. Thus, by 1640hrs, within 15–20 minutes of the Germans advancing from Puisieux Farm, the British had created an ad hoc but strong defensive line of riflemen, machine guns and artillery on Point 109. As soon as the various units of this defensive line had deployed, they independently opened fire on the German dragoons who were about halfway down the opposite slope of the valley. The German accounts express some surprise at the 'violent' and 'heavy' fire they received (Poseck 1921: 73; Vogel 1916: 55; Geßler 1927: 24). Astonishingly, as soon as they came under fire, the two squadrons of the 1. Garde-Dragoner-Regiment dismounted on the exposed forward slope of the northern side of the Vallée de l'Hôtellerie, sent their horses back up the slope towards La Folie Farm, and lying down in the field of root crops, returned fire at the British on the slope above them. According to the regimental history of the 2. Garde-Dragoner-Regiment, Levetzow's 4./2. GDR, which was the rearmost German squadron, simply turned about and calmly trotted back up the slope and over the crest without suffering any casualties (Geßler 1927: 24). The 12th Lancers' machine-gun section turned its fire on the mass of horses from the dismounted squadrons, being led back up the slope. The horse-holders rapidly lost control of the horses which, galled by the Maxim fire, soon stampeded and disappeared over the northern ridgeline of the valley, leaving the German dragoons without mounts, and exposed to the heavy fire of the British.

To the British such an act of folly on the part of the German cavalry was completely inexplicable. Whatever the reason for dismounting, after exchanging fire with the British, the Germans soon realized that further advance was impossible, and the order was given for them to withdraw back up the slope to the supporting troops around La Folie and Puisieux farms.

A German Modell 1889 *Kavalleriedegen*. Its blade is 81cm (32in) long. (© Royal Armouries IX.7677)

Hubertus von Geßler

Hubertus von Geßler was born in Schoffschütz, Germany (now Sowczyce, Poland) on 3 November 1863. He rose through the ranks of the Imperial German Army and as a *Major* was appointed to the command of the prestigious 2. Garde-Dragoner-Regiment, leading his unit to war in 1914. Geßler is recorded as having suffered an accident on 5 December 1915, but he survived World War I and was the author of the regimental history of his former command, published in Oldenburg in 1927. Geßler died in Berlin on 1 February 1934.

In his book, Geßler claimed that the German decision to dismount at Cerizy–Moÿ was taken because the ground was boggy, with the implication that it would impede a cavalry charge, and further stated that the British had erected wire entanglements in front of their position (Geßler 1927: 24). Neither of these claims

is correct. The British had no wire entanglements, although C Sqn Scots Greys was positioned under cover of a hedgerow and a copse. As to the ground being too boggy for cavalry, the dampness of the soil on the valley floor did not hinder the Scots Greys when the regiment charged across the valley a short while later. Nevertheless, there must be some reason why the Germans acted as they did, especially as it was contrary to their training and doctrine, which emphasized the mounted charge with the *arme blanche*. The most plausible explanation would seem to be that the German squadron commanders did truly believe that the terrain or situation was unsuitable for a mounted charge but were determined to assault the British as ordered and, thus, decided to continue the attack on foot.

In the exchange of fire between the dismounted dragoons and C Sqn Scots Greys, Swetenham was killed and Second Lieutenant Sir Gawaine Baillie and six men were wounded. The 12th Lancers, in the regimental war diary, also acknowledged that the carbine fire of the dismounted Germans was steady and accurate. Despite their perilous exposed position, therefore, the dragoons were not panicked but carried out an orderly withdrawal to the crest of the hill behind them while maintaining a steady fire at the British all the time.

Shortly before 3 Sec J Bty RHA came into action, A Sqn and B Sqn 12th Lancers arrived behind the position taken up by C Sqn 12th Lancers. Wormald, who had noticed the dismounted squadrons of the 3. Garde-Kavallerie-Brigade assembling to the east of Puisieux, ordered the two squadrons to move to the high ground on the Germans' left flank and by engaging them with dismounted fire, to prevent them from reinforcing the dragoons in their exposed position in the Vallée de l'Hôtellerie. The two British squadrons at once set off, making use of the dead ground provided by the Vallée de Puisieux to outflank the Germans. As soon as they were in position, they established signal communication with regimental headquarters. At this point Chetwode, who had been absent at a I Corps conference, arrived. He was quickly apprised of the situation and approved of Wormald's decision to commit the brigade reserve to action, which had effectively committed the whole brigade to action. Chetwode ordered 1 Sec J Bty RHA to reinforce 3 Sec, while 2 Sec remained in reserve. He also sent orders to the 20th Hussars to push forward on the British left flank. The dismounted rifle fire of A Sqn and B Sqn 12th Lancers effectively prevented the dismounted squadrons of the 2. Garde-Dragoner-Regiment from intervening to support their comrades withdrawing up the slope towards Puisieux Farm.

The two squadrons of German dragoons had, by this time, withdrawn to the northern crest of the Vallée de l'Hôtellerie and were returning fire at the British. According to all the German accounts, the dragoon squadrons

Frank Wormald

Born in Dewsbury, Yorkshire, on 10 February 1868, Frank Wormald was educated at Harrow and served in the Militia before joining the 12th Lancers in 1889. He attained the rank of lieutenant in 1891 and became a captain in 1898, serving with distinction during the Second Anglo-Boer War. A renowned hunter and polo player, Wormald was appointed CO 12th Lancers in 1912, and led his command to war in 1914.

After being wounded at Cerizy–Moÿ, Wormald was invalided home for three weeks before returning to active service. He was given command of the 5th Cavalry Brigade in August 1915 with the temporary rank of brigadier-general. While inspecting front-line trenches near Vermelles on 3 October 1915, Wormald was killed by a German shell. He is buried in Nedonchel churchyard, Pas-de-Calais, France.

were now ordered to retire back to their horses near La Folie Farm, but this order did not reach the *Zug* from 4./1. GDR commanded by Leutnant Graf von Schwerin on the left flank. This body of men, about 40 in number, had remained lying down and shooting across the valley. The 2. Garde-Dragoner-Regiment sent Leutnant Graf Finck von Finckenstein, the regimental equitation officer, forward to Schwerin's *Zug* to find out what the situation was (Geßler 1927: 24).

Once A Sqn and B Sqn 12th Lancers were in position on the German flank, Wormald instructed C Sqn to mount-up and also to move round the German flank with a view to dismounting closer to the German position and engaging them once more with rifle fire. He sent Captain Charles Bryant, his adjutant, ahead to reconnoitre the ground. While doing this Bryant realized that there was a gully that was not visible to the Germans, but which would allow the British lancers to get within about 50yd (46m) of the enemy unobserved. He reported this fact to Wormald and suggested that it provided an ideal opportunity for shock action. Wormald agreed and, in order to conserve the horses for the charge, led C Sqn at a walk under cover of dead ground to the gully that Bryant had discovered. Wormald ordered the squadron to form line of troop columns as they ascended the gully and, as soon as the Germans came in sight, ordered, 'Gallop. Charge', both signals being given by Trumpet Major William Mowlam in regimental headquarters and taken up by Trumpeter Cousins of C Sqn. As they crested the lip of the gully out of which they were charging, the British lancers gave a cheer. The German dragoons immediately reacted to this sudden and unexpected onslaught; and while one or two remained prone on the ground and another couple raised their hands in surrender, the majority leapt to their feet and turned to shoot at the charging lancers. This was remarkable, given that the British lancers were among them within 20 seconds of charging out of the gully. The 12th Lancers regimental headquarters group, consisting of Wormald, Bryant, Mowlam and two orderlies, were some 30yd (27m) ahead of C Sqn and received the bulk of the German rifle fire.

Wormald, using a 1912 Officers' Cavalry Sword, stabbed a German dragoon, but the force of the impact as the sword went through the man's body buckled the blade, rendering the weapon useless. Almost simultaneously, both Wormald and his horse were shot, the horse being killed and Wormald wounded. Of Wormald's two orderlies, one, Private Nolan, was shot dead, as

Surprise attack

German view: The German dragoons, who have been shooting at C Sqn Scots Greys across the Vallée de l'Hôtellerie to the right of this image, are responding to the sudden appearance of British lancers charging out of dead ground on their left flank, although some men continue to focus on the heavy fire coming from the British positions across the valley. Leutnant Graf von Schwerin is directing his men to form a defensive line on the threatened flank; but with the British only 50yd (46m) away, there is too little time, and within 10 seconds, the foremost British lancers will be riding over the German position, with the line of C Sqn 12th Lancers sweeping through another 10 seconds later. Nevertheless, in that brief space of time, the German dragoons will manage to shoot down all but one of the leading British cavalrymen: four men from the 12th Lancers regimental headquarters group, approaching on the right, and Captain Michell, cresting the lip of the gully with his sword arm raised, in front of C Sqn. The corn stooks dotted around the German position give cover neither from view nor from fire and prove no obstacle at all to the charging line of British cavalrymen.

British view: As the men of C Sqn 12th Lancers gallop over the lip of the gully, they see on the skyline to their right front the trees around Puisieux Farm where elements of the 2. Garde-Dragoner-Regiment are pinned down by the dismounted rifle fire of the 12th Lancers. In front of them is Schwerin's *Zug* from 4./1. GDR, shooting at the British defensive line across the Vallée de l'Hôtellerie to the left of this image. Well in front of C Sqn is the Regimental Headquarters, led by Lieutenant-Colonel Wormald, with Trumpet Major Mowlam giving the bugle call, 'Charge', and Wormald's two orderlies close behind. On the extreme left is the adjutant, Captain Bryant. On the right, Captain Michell is leading the squadron, closely followed by a troop commander and troop sergeant. The men in the squadron are cheering as they lower their Pattern 1868 lances to bring them to the engage. They are looking quite disorderly, in a mix of shirtsleeves and tunics and some without headgear, because of the haste with which they saddled-up and departed from the château where they have been resting as brigade reserve.

was the horse of Private Casey, the other. Casey managed to pull himself free of his dead horse, withdraw his rifle from its bucket and shoot four Germans in the ensuing mêlée. Mowlam was also wounded, being shot in the thigh. The only one of the regimental headquarters not to be hit was Bryant, the adjutant, who was using an old Pattern 1896 cavalry sword in preference to the 1912 Officers' Cavalry Sword and managed to cut down five Germans with it.

Shortly behind the regimental headquarters was Captain Michell at the head of C Sqn. As he galloped out of the gully his horse was shot from under him. Michell scrambled to his feet but was shot in the head, dying instantly. The British lancers charged through the German dragoons, stabbing with their lances and yelling wildly. Once through the German position, in the absence of a squadron commander, Lieutenant Richard Wyndham Quinn, commanding 3 Troop, rallied C Sqn and immediately led the lancers in a second charge through the dismounted Germans. There were still Germans standing and shooting at the lancers, but most were soon rendered *hors de combat*. Once back at the lip of the gully from which they had charged, C Sqn rallied again and went back through the German position, but there was no more opposition from the dragoons, most of whom had been killed or wounded. Four unwounded Germans were found on the field, hiding among the corn stooks, and were made prisoner. Finckenstein had been killed and Schwerin had been severely wounded; he died of his wounds that night (Vogel 1916: 56). When C Sqn 12th Lancers emerged from the gully onto the German position, A Sqn and B Sqn Scots Greys, which were waiting mounted behind C Sqn's firing line, charged across the Vallée de l'Hôtellerie in support. By the time they arrived, however, there was not much to be done, other than prodding the stooks of corn with their swords in case any Germans were hiding among the sheaves. In the meantime, A Sqn and B Sqn 12th Lancers, supported by the regiment's machine-gun section and J Battery RHA, very effectively prevented the 2. Garde-Dragoner-Regiment at Puisieux Farm from mounting a counter-attack.

The four quick-firing 13-pdr guns of J Bty RHA lifted their fire as the lancers charged into the Germans and, in so doing, fortuitously shelled the wood north of La Folie Farm where the Garde-Schützen-Bataillon was assembling to support the hard-pressed 3. Garde-Kavallerie-Brigade. The British shellfire disrupted this assembly and, according to British estimates, inflicted some 200 casualties. None of the German accounts record such high casualties, however, and it is noteworthy that the Garde-Schützen-Bataillon was used later that evening to capture the town of Urvillers, which entailed house-to-house fighting with the French. It seems unlikely, therefore, that the unit suffered such high casualties as the British thought. This raises an interesting point about the reliability of claims regarding casualties inflicted on an enemy. For example, all of the British accounts, including the respective unit war diaries, claim that over 70 dead and wounded Germans were counted on the field of combat after C Sqn's charge. The 1. Garde-Dragoner-Regiment regimental history, however, records a total of 43 casualties from 1. and 4./1. GDR combined, of whom 11 were killed in action or died of their wounds or were missing, 26 were wounded and six were captured (Watson 2016: 111). The 2. Garde-Dragoner-Regiment records Finckenstein as the unit's only casualty. It is impossible to reconcile the German records

In 1914 the British cavalry had two lances in service: The Pattern 1868 lance had a bamboo haft, weighed on average 4lb 2oz (1.9kg), and was 9ft (2.5m) long. The Pattern 1894 lance (shown here) had an ash wood haft, weighed about 5lb (2.3kg), and was 9ft 1in (2.8m) long. Both patterns had the same 5½in (14cm) steel blade. It is not clear which pattern lance the 12th Lancers were using in 1914. (© Royal Armouries PR.1633)

British lancers cross a bridge in France. Where streams or rivers were unfordable by cavalry, bridges became tactically important features. This photo clearly shows one of the great disadvantages of having to rely on bridges, as they channelled movement and forced cavalry formations to bunch up and slow down, making them vulnerable to enemy fire. (The Print Collector/Print Collector/Getty Images)

with the British claims, apparently based on a body-count on the field of combat. Likewise, the Germans claimed to have inflicted heavy casualties on the 20th Hussars when that unit was shelled by Batterie Graf Roedern. The British regiment's war diary, however, records a total casualty count of nine men wounded. It seems, therefore, that both sides greatly overestimated the number of casualties they inflicted on the enemy and, hence, the effect that they had had on enemy morale. Thus, all claims regarding casualties inflicted on the enemy, or that enemy units had been rendered combat ineffective or demoralized, should be treated with the greatest reserve, unless enemy records confirm them.

While the three centre squadrons of the 3. Garde-Kavallerie-Brigade were attempting their mounted attack, 2./2. GDR and 5./1. GDR had advanced down the western side of the RN 44 and occupied some high ground from which Batterie Graf Roedern could shell the British defensive line and support the mounted charge. From the German accounts it is not clear where exactly this battery was located, but based on the British accounts, it seems most likely that the German guns were on Point 119 adjacent to the woods by Lambay Farm. The 20th Hussars, minus A Sqn, had been guarding the British left flank at La Guignette and Cerizy. The hussars were now ordered forward by Chetwode. Leaving Lieutenant Daniel Peploe's troop in Cerizy, the rest of B Sqn along with C Sqn advanced ½ mile (0.8km) north of La Guignette to a ridge from which the dismounted German dragoons and the six 7.7cm field guns of Batterie Graf Roedern on Point 119 were visible. Two troops of C Sqn under Captain Mangles were sent forward to the intervening ridge on Point 116, from which they were to direct dismounted rifle fire on the Germans, while the remaining troop from C Sqn, commanded by Lieutenant Sparrow, was ordered to attempt a mounted attack. It was quickly concluded that a mounted attack was impracticable, and the idea was abandoned. The approach of Sparrow's troop, however, had alerted the Germans to the presence of the 20th Hussars and, in so doing, it certainly diverted the attention of Batterie Graf Roedern from counter-battery fire on J Bty RHA to

the British hussars. Hence, when the remainder of the 20th Hussars attempted to advance mounted around the eastern side of Point 116, Hauptmann Graf Roedern turned his guns on them at a range of some 400yd (366m), causing them to retreat westwards by means of low ground behind Point 116, which masked them from German observation. Consequently, the Germans shelled the RN 44 thoroughly, believing that the 20th Hussars was withdrawing the way it had come. This artillery fire, while completely missing the bulk of the British regiment, did have the effect of stampeding the led horses of the two dismounted troops under Mangles, so that the soldiers of those troops had to retire back towards Cerizy on foot.

At about 1745hrs, the 3. Garde-Kavallerie-Brigade and the Garde-Schützen-Bataillon fell back onto the 2. Garde-Kavallerie-Brigade, which had occupied a ridge about 1½ miles (2.4km) north of Puisieux; the 5th Cavalry Brigade was left in possession of the field. Horse-drawn ambulances from the 5th Cavalry Field Ambulance came forward to collect the wounded of both sides. Some wounded soldiers of the 1. Garde-Dragoner-Regiment managed to hide themselves in a sunken road near La Folie Farm to avoid capture. They were later able to re-join their regiment. The British medics did what they could for the wounded but were unable to provide advanced medical care, which would have required evacuation to a hospital. The more severely wounded German and British soldiers, including Trumpet Major Mowlam, therefore, had to be left behind in Moÿ when the 5th Cavalry Brigade resumed its southerly withdrawal around 2130hrs that night. These men fell into German hands the next day, when some of the Germans complained at what they felt was the poor medical treatment they had received from the British (Vogel 1916: 56).

The Germans advanced no further for the rest of the day. On the night of 28/29 August, the Garde-Kavallerie-Division billeted around Essigny-le-Grand and Urvillers. While Urvillers was being secured by the Garde-Schützen-Bataillon, the 2. Garde-Dragoner-Regiment cleared the wood around La Folie Farm, recovering a number of wounded dragoons from the 1. Garde-Dragoner-Regiment. On returning from this task, the German cavalrymen heard shooting to the north, so the regiment sent patrols to ascertain what was happening in its rear. It transpired that elements of the 5. Kavallerie-Division, which was billeting around Itancourt, had become confused in the dark and had fired upon each other (Geßler 1927: 25).

Two sections of J Bty RHA. This battery did sterling service at Cerizy and, by shelling the assembly area of the Garde-Schützen-Bataillon, undoubtedly turned the tide of battle in favour of the British. (Chronicle/Alamy Stock Photo)

Le Montcel

7 September 1914

BACKGROUND TO BATTLE

On 29 August the BEF continued its wearying retreat pursued by Kluck's 1. Armee. Generaloberst Karl von Bülow's 2. Armee hammered Lanrezac's V Armée, forcing it back. On 30 August Bülow asked for Kluck's support in order to destroy the V Armée. Kluck ordered his forces to wheel south-eastwards, leaving General der Artillerie Hans von Gronau's IV. Reservekorps and the 4. Kavallerie-Division to guard his exposed right flank. This meant that Kluck's 1. Armee, which had been aiming for the Seine River west of Paris with the intention of enveloping and capturing the French capital, now

German dragoons charge down a slope during manoeuvres. Note how the riders are leaning back in the saddle as they descend the slope. In 1914 cavalrymen of all of the European armies, barring Italy, were trained to lean back like this when jumping obstacles or descending slopes, as it was believed that this helped the horse to retain its centre of balance. Nowadays, riders schooled in the 'Forward Seat' believe that leaning back in this way actually hinders the horse and adopt a very different posture when jumping or riding downhill. (SZ Photo/Süddeutsche Zeitung Photo/Alamy Stock Photo)

swung towards the south-east and bypassed Paris to its south. The Germans had effectively abandoned the Schlieffen Plan and, in so doing, they lost their only chance of capturing Paris and knocking France out of the war.

As Joffre awaited the right moment for a decisive counter-attack, the BEF and the V Armée continued their withdrawal east of Paris, thus drawing the 1. and 2. Armeen deeper into his trap. On 5 September, as the advancing Germans exposed their right flank to the forces assembled in Paris, Joffre ordered VI Armée, the BEF and the V Armée to launch the counter-offensive. Général Michel-Joseph Maunoury began to push his newly constituted VI Armée eastwards from Paris, only to be halted by the IV. Reservekorps. Seeing the danger of an attack from the VI Armée on his exposed right flank Kluck ordered the IX. and III. Armeekorps to move north-westwards from his left flank across to his right flank, leaving a 25-mile (40km)-wide gap between his 1. Armee and Bülow's 2. Armee, which was to be covered by HKK 1.

On the evening of 6 September the Garde-Kavallerie-Division, which was west of Bülow's 2. Armee, went into billets at Beton-Bazoches, some 50 miles (80km) east of Paris. First thing on the morning of 7 September the staff officers in the Garde-Kavallerie-Division headquarters were confidently predicting that by evening they would be dining in Fontainebleau Palace, some 40 miles (64km) further south-west on the Seine. By 0800hrs, however, this optimism was shaken by a series of events.

First, at 0500hrs the staff officers at HKK 1 learned that the IX. and III. Armeekorps of the 1. Armee had apparently begun to retreat north-westwards and that HKK 1 was ordered to cover their withdrawal and then itself to withdraw north across the Petit Morin River. Second, as Joffre's counter-offensive began to develop, the Garde-Kavallerie-Division's attached *Jäger* battalions became engaged in heavy fighting south-east of Beton-Bazoches with French troops attacking from the south.

At the same time, Generalleutnant Adolf von Storch, commander of the Garde-Kavallerie-Division, became aware of British cavalry advancing from the west. It quickly became apparent that the Garde-Kavallerie-Division was in danger of being enveloped by an enemy pincer movement from the west and south-east. One of the staff officers who had been so confident just a couple of hours earlier, observed dourly, "Well, God alone can help us!" (Vogel 1916: 84).

A squadron of German dragoons in close order 'squadron column' formation. Drill was a fundamental part of training both horses and men, teaching the horse to stay quietly in the ranks and to conform to the other horses around it. The man also had to learn the intricacies of riding in close formation so that, in the heat of battle, the cavalry squadron could manoeuvre efficiently and effectively against the enemy. (Chronicle/Alamy Stock Photo)

A British cavalry bivouac, 1914. The men and horses of both sides had to adapt quickly to living and bivouacking outdoors. In these conditions, the cavalryman's knowledge of horsemastership was vital to keeping the horses fit and healthy. It was the cavalryman's lot, therefore, to tend to the needs of his remount before seeing to his own. (Daily Mirror/Mirrorpix/Mirrorpix via Getty Images)

As the situation unfolded, therefore, the Garde-Kavallerie-Division ordered the 3. Garde-Kavallerie-Brigade to hold off the advancing enemy in order to allow time for the withdrawal of the division's baggage train. The guns of the *Reiter-Abtheilung* of the 1. Garde-Feldartillerie-Regiment were concentrated at Beton-Bazoches in order to support the division's units as they attempted to extricate themselves from the advancing Allies. The 2. Garde-Dragoner-Regiment was assigned the task of protecting the artillery (Geßler 1927: 36), leaving the 1. Garde-Dragoner-Regiment to act as the flank guard covering the withdrawal of the rest of the division.

At 0700hrs, before the scale of the Allied counter-offensive had become apparent, the 1. Garde-Dragoner-Regiment was ordered to reconnoitre to the west in anticipation of continuing the German advance on the Seine. After a month of hard campaigning the regiment was understrength, mustering only some 400 dragoons on worn-out horses. The German dragoons advanced in double-column along the south bank of the Aubetin stream, which they discovered was not fordable by cavalry (Poseck 1921: 97–98). This fact made the few bridges crossing the stream of tactical importance, as possession of them was essential to permit manoeuvre.

Oberstleutnant Freiherr Max von Holzing-Berstett, the commanding officer of the 1. Garde-Dragoner-Regiment, became aware that enemy cavalry had just occupied Frétoy, so he ordered his regiment to cross from the south to the north side of the Aubetin over the bridge at Grand Frétoy and to occupy La Hutte woods south of La Clottée Farm, about ¾ mile (1.2km) east of Le Montcel. Dismounting and forming a firing line on foot along the western and southern edges of the woodland, 1. and 3./1. GDR sent their horses back to the rear. On the north side of the wood, 4./1. GDR, which could muster only two weak *Züge*, and 5./1. GDR also dismounted but remained with their saddled-up horses. Not counting those detached on patrols, there were about 70 men in 5./1. GDR and some 40 in 4./1. GDR, giving a mounted force of over 100 men available to respond to any contingency. This force increased in strength as various patrols and detachments re-joined their respective squadrons, until 5./1. GDR amounted to about 110 men and 4./1. GDR between 50 and 60 men. Once his regiment was in position, Holzing-Berstett rode into Le Montcel with a small patrol to reconnoitre (Gayling 1920: 30).

The enemy of which they had become aware was the right flank guard of the BEF, the 1st Cavalry Division (as the original Cavalry Division was

A German 'officer patrol' of three dragoons and an officer advances cautiously across country. The men have slung their Kar 98AZ carbines over their shoulders, presumably to make them more accessible, and have discarded their lances, which would simply be a hindrance when scouting. Interestingly, this patrol has adopted the kite-shaped formation advocated by the British cavalry officer Major-General Robert Baden-Powell in the 1909 second edition of his book, *Aids to Scouting for N.C.O's & Men.* Reconnaissance was the primary cavalry role at both strategic and tactical levels and was usually carried out by small officer-led patrols, such as the one pictured here. Nevertheless, successful scouting required soldiers who, in addition to being specially trained, were intelligent, independent and bold without being reckless – qualities that no amount of training could provide. (Scherl/Süddeutsche Zeitung Photo/Alamy Stock Photo)

designated from 15 September, having had the 3rd Cavalry Brigade detached on 5 September). On 7 September the 1st Cavalry Division's orders were to advance via Dagny on Choisy-en-Brie, while the 2nd Cavalry Brigade, the division's right flank guard and the most easterly formation of the BEF, was to advance through Frétoy and Faujus to Choisy-en-Brie. The 2nd Cavalry Brigade bivouacked for the night at Jouy-le-Châtel, some 6 miles (10km) west-south-west of Beton-Bazoches. On 7 September the brigade's regiments resumed their advance, assembling at the brigade rendezvous at Les Essarts-Jonchery at 0630hrs. The 9th Lancers, under the command of Lieutenant-Colonel David Campbell, was appointed brigade vanguard for the day, even though the regiment was understrength by almost 100 men after the heavy losses suffered in the disastrous charge at Audregnies and subsequent skirmishes with the Germans during the retreat from Mons. The 18th Hussars led the main body of the brigade, followed by I Bty RHA, with the 4th Dragoon Guards bringing up the rear (Burnett 1922).

The 9th Lancers left the brigade rendezvous at 0700hrs with Major Eustace Abadie's C Sqn as the lead squadron. Two troops were detached to reconnoitre; one, under Lieutenant George Taylor-Whitehead, scouted east towards Le Mazet, and the other, under Lieutenant Henry Mather-Jackson, was sent north towards Dagny. A Sqn, under Captain Douglas Lucas-Tooth, covered the right flank of the regiment, sending patrols towards Bannost. Some short distance behind C Sqn were the regimental headquarters, the understrength B Sqn and the machine-gun section under Lieutenant Frederick de Vere Allfrey, which had been reduced to one Maxim gun and seven men (Watson 2016: 66f).

Shortly after moving off at 0700hrs, the British patrols made contact with the German vedettes around Frétoy. Quickly appreciating the importance of securing both the crossings over the Aubetin and the tactically important high ground to the north of the stream, Campbell ordered his regiment to secure the village of Frétoy, the bridges over the Aubetin, and less than ½ mile (0.8km) further north, Le Montcel. Exactly as anticipated in pre-war cavalry doctrine, a combat between two cavalry forces acting as flank guards to their respective armies was now imminent.

MAP KEY

1 0700hrs: Having bivouacked at Beton-Bazoches, the 1. Garde-Dragoner-Regiment advances along the south side of the Aubetin stream, crossing to the north bank via the footbridge at Grand Frétoy when it is realized that British cavalry are advancing on Frétoy, and secures La Hutte woods.

2 0700hrs: Having bivouacked just north-east of Jouy-le-Châtel, the 9th Lancers, acting as advanced guard of the 2nd Cavalry Brigade, departs from the brigade rendezvous at Les Essarts-Jonchery and advances towards Frétoy and Le Montcel, pushing back German vedettes as it does so.

3 0730hrs: C Sqn 9th Lancers drives the outpost from the 1. Garde-Dragoner-Regiment out of Le Montcel.

4 *c.*0730hrs: Lieutenant Taylor-Whitehead's troop from A Sqn 9th Lancers skirmishes with a German patrol and then is ordered to secure the heights beyond Le Montcel. Shortly afterwards the troop opens fire on 4. and 5./1. GDR assembled just north of La Hutte woods.

5 *c.*0740hrs: Lieutenant-Colonel Campbell, CO 9th Lancers, positions two troops of B Sqn 9th Lancers behind some haystacks at the north-east corner of the Bois du Montcel.

6 *c.*0745hrs: Brigadier-General de Lisle orders the 18th Hussars to cross the Aubetin, which the regiment does at Ferme Aubetin, and to envelop the northern flank of the 1. Garde-Dragoner-Regiment at La Hutte and La Clottée.

7 0750hrs: 4./1. GDR launches a mounted attack on the 9th Lancers in Le Montcel, causing some of the British cavalrymen to withdraw southwards across the Aubetin.

8 0800hrs: In order to cover the phased withdrawal of the rest of the 1. Garde-Dragoner-Regiment from La Hutte to La Clottée, Rittmeister Gayling von Altheim's 5./1. GDR launches a mounted attack on the two troops of B Sqn 9th Lancers assembled just north-west of Le Montcel. The B Sqn troops mount an immediate counter-charge.

9 0810hrs: After the mêlée, B Sqn 9th Lancers rallies just north of Le Montcel and then withdraws to the south side of the hamlet, pursued by some of 5./1. GDR. The Germans abandon the pursuit on discovering that Le Montcel has been re-occupied by the British.

10 0810hrs: After the mêlée, 5./1. GDR rallies north of the Bois du Montcel and withdraws to La Clottée, leaving Oberleutnant Buddenbruck's *Zug* to secure the field and collect the wounded.

11 0830hrs: A Sqn 18th Hussars dismounts west of the Bois du Montcel and opens fire on Buddenbruck's *Zug*, forcing them to retire towards La Clottée without recovering the German wounded. The dismounted A Sqn 18th Hussars pursues the retreating Germans, advancing towards La Clottée until stopped by German rifle and machine-gun fire.

12 0830hrs: B Sqn 18th Hussars is ordered to swing north towards Faujus in order to envelop the northern flank of the 1. Garde-Dragoner-Regiment's defensive position at La Clottée. The British cavalrymen ride to just south of Faujus without being seen, dismount and, leaving one troop with the led horses, the other three troops advance on foot towards La Clottée from the north.

13 0845hrs: The 1. Garde-Dragoner-Regiment squadrons stage a phased withdrawal to Les Hayottes. Oberstleutnant Holzing-Berstett, commanding officer of the 1. Garde-Dragoner-Regiment, sees the led horses of B Sqn 18th Hussars and orders 4./1. GDR to charge and drive off the British.

14 0900hrs: 4./1. GDR attempts a mounted attack on the three dismounted troops of B Sqn 18th Hussars, but is repulsed with very heavy losses.

15 0900hrs: I Bty RHA moves into position north of Le Montcel to provide artillery support to the 2nd Cavalry Brigade and begins to shell Les Hayottes, but without causing much damage to the Germans.

Battlefield environment

Monday 7 September 1914 was hazy, which reduced visibility to the extent that A Sqn 18th Hussars was able to deploy in the open only 300yd (274m) from Oberleutnant Buddenbruck's *Zug* without the Germans noticing. By 0930hrs the day had turned hot, and the temperature had soared.

The Aubetin stream, running almost west–east from Beton-Bazoches, lay in a fairly steep-sided valley (Coleman 1916: 94). The countryside on either side was undulating and dotted with scattered woodland among fields of harvested corn and other crops (Burnett 1922; Poseck 1921). Some of the woodland was bounded by wire fences, which had to be cut to allow passage for the horses (Burnett 1922). Both sides took advantage of the

wooded, undulating terrain to manoeuvre. For example, the Germans used a shallow re-entrant running north-east between La Clottée and Les Hayottes as a covered route by which to withdraw from La Clottée. Likewise, the 18th Hussars were able to move unseen between Moneuse and Faujus. Although distant observation was difficult, the two cavalry charges both took place on open, flat fields with unrestricted visibility at close ranges. There were no obstacles, such as wire fencing, at either site that would hinder a mounted cavalry charge.

The villages around which the fighting occurred were small hamlets. The Germans made use of the farmsteads, surrounded by strong stone walls, as defensive points.

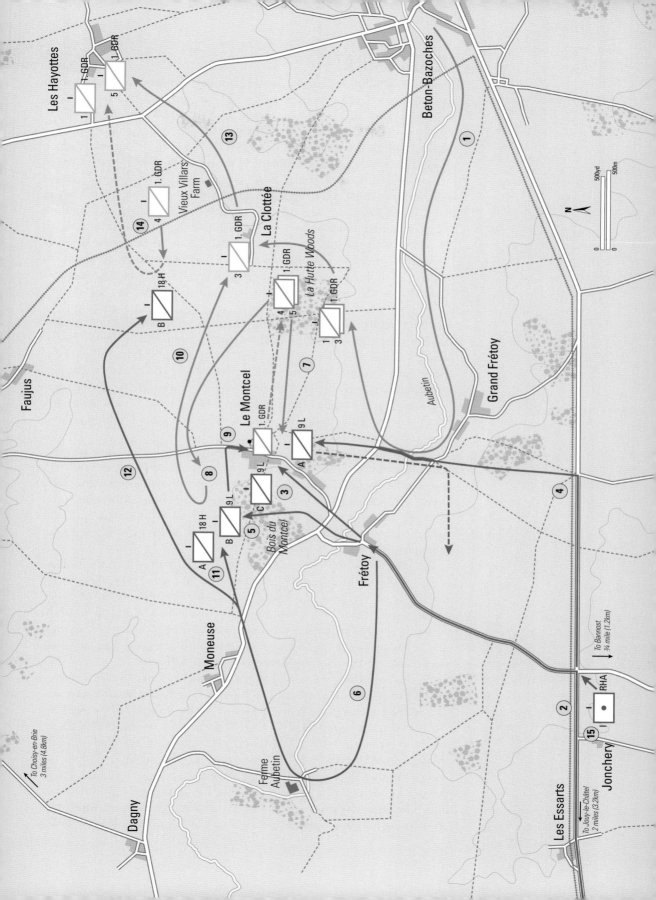

Les Hayottes

1·GDR

1·GDR
5

13

1·GDR
4
Vieux Villars
Farm

14

La Clottée

1·GDR
3

1·GDR
4 5
La Hutte Woods

1·GDR
1 3

7

18 H
B

10

9

Le Montcel

1·GDR

9 L
A

9 L
C

3

9 L
B

5

Bois du
Montcel

18 H
A

11

12

8

Faujus

Moneuse

Dagny

To Choisy-en-Brie
3 miles (4.8km)

Frétoy

Ferme
Aubetin

6

Beton-Bazoches

1

Grand Frétoy

Aubetin

4

To Bannost
¾ mile (1.2km)

RHA

2

15

Jonchery

Les Essarts

To Jouy-le-Châtel
2 miles (3.2km)

500yd
500m

N

INTO COMBAT

Soon after 0700hrs on 7 September the screen of German vedettes and patrols around Frétoy and Le Montcel began to be driven back by the advancing British cavalry. Taylor-Whitehead and his troop encountered a German cavalry patrol on the road north of Bannost, which, after opening fire on the British, withdrew northwards towards Frétoy. At about 0745hrs a German outpost that had occupied Le Montcel the previous evening was surprised when a mounted troop from C Sqn 9th Lancers suddenly swept down the main street of the hamlet, forcing them to withdraw onto the main body of the 1. Garde-Dragoner-Regiment in La Hutte woods. The rest of C Sqn was soon committed in skirmishes with German patrols around Le Montcel.

Shortly after the lead troop from C Sqn 9th Lancers cleared Le Montcel, Taylor-Whitehead was ordered to take his understrength troop across the Aubetin east of Frétoy and occupy the heights to the north-east of Le Montcel. They crossed the Aubetin by the footbridge at Grand Frétoy and, skirting Le Montcel on their left, soon saw 4. and 5./1. GDR massed north of La Hutte woods. The presence of the Germans was reported, but Campbell did not receive this report, as shall become apparent. At this point Taylor-Whitehead had only two men with him – it is not clear what had happened to the rest of his troop – when he was joined by Abadie and, shortly afterwards, by another five men (Taylor-Whitehead, cited in Watson 2016: 70). The men who joined them included Farrier Sergeant Swain who, with a few others, had been delayed in saddling-up first thing in the morning and had been pressing on to try to re-join the regiment.

It is an indication of how confused the situation was and how scattered the various troops of the 9th Lancers were, that this party of laggards suddenly ended up at the front of the regiment's position without having encountered any of their comrades en route. Among those with Swain had been Private (Shoeing Smith) Arthur Friend. Somehow, Friend became separated from the others and ended up going into Le Montcel on his own, where he was subsequently killed.

Abadie sent Swain alone to the north end of Le Montcel to guard the flank of this small party of lancers, while he himself went back to bring the scattered remainder of his squadron up to join Taylor-Whitehead's party. Swain encountered a patrol of five mounted Germans in Le Montcel, at which he promptly opened fire, causing them to withdraw from the village. He thought that he had hit two of the Germans. It is possible that this German patrol was the detachment that Holzing-Berstett took into the hamlet.

In the meantime, the small party under Taylor-Whitehead had opened fire on the massed men of 4. and 5./1. GDR. The Germans, after returning fire, decided to charge the British position. Having returned to his regiment, Holzing-Berstett had ordered 5./1. GDR to advance on the British lancers visible to the north-west of Le Montcel. It is probable, therefore, that the two squadrons that Taylor-Whitehead records as charging him, were the two understrength *Züge* of 4./1. GDR. One of these swung north and rode straight through Le Montcel past Swain, clearing the hamlet of the few British soldiers in it. The other *Zug* made straight for Taylor-Whitehead's party, which kept on shooting until the Germans were only about 70yd (64m) away, at which

German cavalry supply train, escorted by dragoons. The two wagons in the foreground are mobile field kitchens. It was the necessity of permitting the slow-moving supply train of the Garde-Kavallerie-Division to withdraw unmolested across the Grand Morin River that led the 1. Garde-Dragoner-Regiment to being ordered to cover the Garde-Kavallerie-Division's western flank and resulted in the combat around Le Montcel. (Süddeutsche Zeitung Photo/Alamy Stock Photo)

point the British lancers mounted-up and withdrew, pursued by the German dragoons. Taylor-Whitehead had to jump his horse over a barbed-wire fence to escape one of the pursuing Germans, who nearly managed to stab him with his lance. The small party of 9th Lancers were forced to retreat back across the footbridge at Grand Frétoy and rallied at a small copse south-east of Frétoy, while the Germans re-joined their regiment at La Hutte. Taylor-Whitehead then led his men back into Le Montcel after the Germans had retired (Taylor-Whitehead, cited in Watson 2016: 70).

Campbell had followed close behind C Sqn. Coming across Abadie in Le Montcel, he ordered him to secure the high ground north of the hamlet with his squadron, but Abadie replied that he had no men available as they were all engaged in skirmishes with the Germans. Campbell, therefore, rode back to Frétoy and brought the two understrength troops of B Sqn, the regimental headquarters and the machine-gun section across the Aubetin at Frétoy, and then, taking them cross-country west of Le Montcel, halted them behind some haystacks at the north-east corner of the Bois du Montcel. Hearing rifle fire coming from the direction of Le Montcel, Campbell rode into the hamlet with his trumpeter to find out what was happening. He soon saw Taylor-Whitehead's party shooting towards the east but, because of the haze, he could not see what they were shooting at. Leaving his trumpeter, Campbell rode towards La Hutte woods on his own in order to ascertain what his men were shooting at. The fact that he did this indicates that he had not received the reports from his patrols stating that there was a body of German cavalry massed north of the wood.

When Campbell was some 400yd (366m) from La Hutte, he saw about 100 German cavalry mounting up and beginning to trot towards him in column of troops formation. He immediately turned around and galloped back to B Sqn. Campbell was well-mounted on a fresh horse, so he quickly left the German squadron behind, and when he re-joined B Sqn the Germans were still some 800yd (732m) away. As he rode back towards his men he weighed up whether to meet the advancing Germans with dismounted rifle fire or a mounted counter-charge. He decided to adopt the latter course of action as he felt that it would be good for his men's morale (Campbell, cited in Watson 2016: 71–72).

Holzing-Berstett had returned from his reconnaissance of Le Montcel, having seen the two troops of B Sqn 9th Lancers in their position by the haystacks near the Bois du Montcel. On his return to the 1. Garde-Dragoner-Regiment, he also received reports from his patrols that Allied infantry were advancing on Faujus, a village some 1¼ miles (2km) to the north. Realizing that they posed a threat of interdicting the withdrawing Garde-Kavallerie-Division baggage train, Holzing-Berstett decided to implement a phased fighting withdrawal by occupying a series of defensible positions around La Clottée, Vieux Villars and Les Hayottes, strongly walled farms to the north of La Hutte and east of Faujus. The British cavalry he had seen at Le Montcel, however, were an immediate threat that might prevent the 1. Garde-Dragoner-Regiment from carrying out this manoeuvre. In order to buy time for the withdrawal, he ordered Rittmeister Freiherr Carl Gayling von Altheim and 5./1. GDR to charge the British cavalry (Poseck 1921: 98). (Some accounts give Gayling's squadron as 2./1. GDR. In fact, on the outbreak of war, the squadrons were renumbered in order to create a reserve squadron that remained in Germany; 2./1. GDR then became 5./1. GDR.) It was this squadron of about 100 men that Campbell had seen advancing from La Hutte woods and which he had decided to counter-charge.

The German accounts state that the British lancers simply sat on their horses, apparently waiting motionless to receive their charge, which puzzled the dragoons (Gayling 1920: 30; Poseck 1921: 98). When the Germans first sighted B Sqn, they were indeed stationary, waiting in column of troops formation where Campbell had placed them, but they were soon put in motion. Sergeant Taylor of B Sqn recalled that when Campbell reached the two troops of B Sqn, about 40 men in all, he simply said, 'Follow me, gentlemen,' and brought them out from behind the haystacks where they had been sheltering. The German dragoons were now about 700yd (640m) distant and Captain Guy Reynolds, the adjutant, said in amazement, 'By God, Colonel, they're going to charge us!' (Taylor, cited in Watson 2016: 74).

As soon as Campbell ordered B Sqn to follow him, Allfrey and the machine-gun section set up the Maxim gun near the northern edge of Le Montcel and opened fire on the advancing German squadron, which was still in column of troops formation. Sergeant Mehlis, on the left wing of 5./1. GDR, realizing the danger of enfilading fire from the machine gun, immediately took six men and charged the Maxim. Oberleutnant Freiherr von Buddenbruck, the *Zug* commander, quickly followed Mehlis with the rest of the *Zug*. The gun crew fell back before the charging Germans, who captured the Maxim gun. As they could not carry the gun away, the dragoons struck its mechanism with stones. Buddenbruck and his men then rode further into Le Montcel, which they later described as full of British troops, who opened fire on the Germans. Dragoner de Ries was killed; and Buddenbruck recalled hacking at a dismounted British officer, whom he described as 'a bold fellow', with his sword, slashing him across the head and face (Poseck 1921: 99). It is likely that this was not an officer but Private (Shoeing Smith) Friend, who was found after the battle with his head smashed in. Buddenbruck quickly withdrew his troop by way of the north exit from the hamlet (Gayling 1920: 30; Poseck 1921: 99). The 9th Lancers' machine-gun section returned to the Maxim gun, but could not fire it as the Germans had jammed it when they tried to smash the mechanism.

Coming under fire from the 9th Lancers' machine-gun section, Gayling ordered his dragoons to deploy into an extended line and then gave the signal for them to increase their pace to the gallop. As their horses were worn out after a month of campaigning, they were simply unable to attain the regulation gallop (15mph; 24km/h) and so the charge was delivered at the slower pace of the canter (about 12mph; 19km/h).

Having brought his men out in column of troops formation, Campbell gave the order, "Left wheel into line. Gallop!" (Campbell, cited in Anglesey 1996: 186). The British lancers spurred their horses into the regulation gallop pace of 15mph (24km/h) towards the oncoming Germans, which meant that the two converging forces would cover the distance separating them in less than a minute (*Cavalry Training 1912*: §52.1). The lancers, therefore, did not have time to form ranks properly or adopt the knee-to-knee line prescribed in the drill books. Instead, they formed a ragged irregular line with more spacing between the horses than was usual in a charge. As the Germans had at least twice as many men as the British, the frontage of their squadron line was about twice as wide as the frontage covered by the two troops of British lancers. The latter simply directed their counter-charge at the nearest part of the German squadron, i.e. the left half of the German line. Seeing the British half-squadron in front of him, Gayling ordered his squadron to wheel diagonally to their left in order to close ranks and to meet the British head-on, but on their already jaded horses, the right wing could not increase pace sufficiently in order to effect this simple manoeuvre (Gayling 1920: 30). Consequently, when the German and British squadrons met each other, they were both in a more extended order than that prescribed in the drill books.

The British eyewitness accounts agree that the British counter-charged at a much faster pace than that of the Germans (Coleman 1916: 96; Vaughan 1954: 165). Nevertheless, Campbell, who was on a fresh horse and had been an amateur jockey in his younger days, realized to his dismay when he was about 100yd (91m) from the German line that he had left his men well behind and that they were still some 100yd behind him.

Campbell, therefore, encountered the German line on his own. With his revolver, he shot at a German *Zug* commander who was cutting at his head with his *Kavalleriedegen* and was then stabbed in the arm by a German lance and lifted out of the saddle, falling backwards over the croup of his horse. Shortly behind Campbell came Reynolds, also on his own, who was promptly unseated by a German lance and severely wounded in the shoulder. The lance was torn from the German dragoon's hand and Reynolds fell to the earth with the lance still through his shoulder. The next moment both German and British troopers rode over and around the prostrate Campbell but, amazingly, not a horse trod on him as he lay on the ground.

PREVIOUS PAGES

Lance against lance

Having come under fire from the 9th Lancers' machine-gun section, Rittmeister Freiherr Gayling von Altheim has ordered 5./1. GDR to deploy into an extended line and given the signal for the dragoons to increase their pace to the gallop. The two troops of B Sqn 9th Lancers have come out from behind some haystacks, just off-screen to the right of this image, and have left-wheeled into line to counter-charge the Germans. Ahead of the British line is Lieutenant-Colonel Campbell, CO 9th Lancers, aiming for the German *Zug* commander, visible in the centre of the image. The Germans, seeing Campbell approaching, are in the act of couching their lances even though the bulk of the British force is still just over 100yd (91m) distant. Midway between Campbell and B Sqn is the adjutant, Captain Reynolds, holding his Webley revolver aloft.

Sick, injured or wounded horses required medical treatment just as much as the men. Each cavalry division had a mobile veterinary section attached to it. In this photo British veterinary personnel treat an injured horse, France, 11 November 1914. (Daily Mirror/Mirrorpix/Mirrorpix via Getty Images)

The British brought their lances to the engage when about 50yd (46m) from the Germans. According to Lance Corporal Hunt of C Sqn 9th Lancers, who witnessed the action from Le Montcel, there was a wild yell just before the two converging lines of cavalrymen met (Hunt, cited in Watson 2016: 75), probably because British cavalrymen were trained to cheer just before impact when they charged (*Cavalry Training 1912*: §204.8), but also because of the natural instinct in all men to yell when engaging an enemy hand-to-hand. Campbell, lying wounded on the ground, records that the Germans were also shouting at the tops of their voices (Campbell, cited in Watson 2016: 77). Taylor, who participated in the charge, recalled that there was a resounding crash when the two forces met, as horses collided, lances clashed, and men were knocked out of the saddle (Taylor, cited in Watson 2016: 74). Interestingly, none of the horses on either side refused at the moment of impact, and all charged home (Coleman 1916: 96).

The fact that neither side was charging knee to knee may have contributed to this. Squadron Sergeant Major Hugh Durant's horse collided with that of a German dragoon, both horses rearing up, and he was thrown to the ground where he received five lance wounds, leaving him badly injured. It is claimed, however, that he managed to shoot a number of Germans with his semi-automatic pistols before he was unseated from his horse (Campbell, cited in Watson 2016: 78).

When the two sides collided, there was inevitably a degree of confusion as the opposing lines rode through each other and a short mêlée developed. The lance of one sergeant in the 9th Lancers went straight through his German opponent until his hand

A German cavalry outpost near Bayonville, France. These cavalrymen, both NCOs, are probably from one of the reserve or Landwehr cavalry regiments, as they are still armed with the older Modell 1898 cavalry carbine, which had been replaced in 1908 with the much more effective Kar 98AZ carbine for the regiments of the standing army. (Author's Collection)

hit the German's chest, being spattered with blood. A British NCO stabbed a German officer or NCO with his lance while, at the same moment, the German severed the British soldier's hand with his *Kavalleriedegen*. One German dragoon was pinned to the back of his horse by a British lance; the horse then galloped around the field trying to dislodge its rider (Coleman 1916: 97; de Lisle 1939: 137). Private Sage of the 9th Lancers, having unseated one German dragoon in the initial collision, was soon hemmed in by three dragoons, one of whom stabbed him in the back with his lance-butt, knocking him off his horse. One of the dragoons then killed his horse with a lance-thrust, which Sage thought unsporting. Sergeant Wyness engaged in a sword duel with a German officer or NCO, the result being Wyness's horse received a bad cut behind the saddle, but neither man managed to harm the other. The duel ended when the German disengaged and cantered away (Sage, cited in Watson 2016: 74). Taylor unseated a German dragoon with his sword but, at the same time, the dragoon stabbed Taylor's horse with his lance, giving it a wound from which it subsequently died. Lance Corporal Bolke ran his lance through a dismounted German who had his hands raised in surrender, which Taylor deprecated (Taylor, cited in Watson 2016: 74–75).

The mêlée was short, however, as both sides rode through each other's lines and continued onwards. Major Desmond Beale-Browne rallied the British lancers and led them onto the road back into Le Montcel. Taylor's wounded horse reached the road before it collapsed, falling on top of Taylor, and pinning him to the ground. A German dragoon galloping down the road stabbed Taylor in the back with his lance as he passed (Taylor, cited in Watson 2016: 75).

Gayling also quickly rallied his squadron just short of the Bois du Montcel and led them back across the field of combat towards La Clottée Farm, to which the rest of the 1. Garde-Dragoner-Regiment had withdrawn from La Hutte woods. Gayling ordered Buddenbruck to take his *Zug* back to recover any German casualties on the field. While doing this, some of the dragoons began to go through the pockets of the injured British soldiers, including those of the badly wounded Reynolds who still had a German lance impaled in his shoulder. Buddenbruck and his men, however, were soon driven off the field by rifle fire from the 18th Hussars, who had circled round to the north side of the Bois du Montcel, and were forced to leave their wounded to be captured by the British (Vogel 1916: 86). As the Germans withdrew, Allfrey, the 9th Lancers' machine-gun officer, ran forward from the hamlet to try to pull the lance from Reynolds' shoulder, but was shot and killed by a wounded German lying on the field.

Once Gayling's squadron had re-traversed the combat site, Campbell stood up and, seeing one of his men approaching from Le Montcel, took his horse and rode southwards between the hamlet and the Bois du Montcel in order to report what had happened to Brigadier-General Henry de Lisle. En route, Campbell was wounded again, being shot in the leg by a German who was in Le Montcel (Campbell, cited in Watson 2016: 77). This may have been one of Buddenbruck's *Zug*, or it could have been one of the wounded Germans who had entered the hamlet after the charge, or it could have been the unwounded German dragoon who shortly afterwards was found hiding in the orchard just north-west of Le Montcel (Coleman 1916: 97). It is a measure of the fluidity of the situation that both British and German cavalrymen either singly or in small parties seem to have been wandering around Le Montcel and its environs willy-nilly.

In the meantime, de Lisle, seeing the 9th Lancers held up in Le Montcel, ordered Lieutenant-Colonel Charles Burnett, CO 18th Hussars, to take A Sqn and B Sqn of his regiment, cross the Aubetin to the west of Frétoy, and move his men into position to envelop the German right flank. The 18th Hussars found a crossing at Ferme Aubetin about 1 mile (1.6km) west of Frétoy and, once on the north side of the Aubetin, advanced east through woodland, emerging just south of the hamlet of Moneuse. They crossed to the north of the Dagny–Le Montcel road in order to come round the northern edge of the Bois du Montcel. Scouts reported that there were German cavalry on the plain ahead. Burnett and Major Stewart, OC A Sqn 18th Hussars, went forward to see for themselves and some 500yd (457m) distant, saw 30–40 men of Buddenbruck's *Zug*, dismounted on the field of combat. Burnett ordered Stewart to send one of his troops into Le Montcel and secure it, while the other two troops were dismounted and formed a firing line running north–south north of the Bois du Montcel. At a range of about 300yd (274m) the British hussars opened rapid fire on the Germans, causing some casualties and compelling them to withdraw towards Vieux Villars. The dismounted hussars followed Buddenbruck's *Zug* on foot for about 1,000yd (914m) until they came under fire from the rest of the 1. Garde-Dragoner-Regiment at La Clottée Farm (Burnett 1922). With Le Montcel now in British hands, de Lisle ordered I Bty RHA to cross the Aubetin at Frétoy and to move into a firing position just north of Le Montcel. It was shortly after 0900hrs.

While A Sqn 18th Hussars secured Le Montcel and pushed on towards La Clottée and Vieux Villars from the west, Burnett ordered B Sqn under Major Charles Leveson to move north under cover of some wooded undulating country towards Faujus with a view to enveloping the Germans at La Clottée

and cutting them off from Vieux Villars Farm. Leveson led his squadron to a position ¾ mile (1.2km) south of Faujus, keeping them mounted until the last possible moment. Here the hussars dismounted and Captain Frank Sopper, the squadron second-in-command, was left among some trees with one weak troop to guard the led horses. The other three troops, also very understrength, set off on foot to attack La Clottée from the north-west.

Holzing-Berstett had now to extract his regiment from the precarious position in which it found itself while at the same time still covering the retirement of the Garde-Kavallerie-Division. He was confident that the charge of 5./1. GDR had, for the moment, stopped the British cavalry advancing from Frétoy but he had still to delay the British infantry advancing on Faujus. He therefore planned a phased withdrawal of his regiment from La Clottée to Les Hayottes. Rittmeister von Schlick and his very weak 3./1. GDR were ordered to defend La Clottée for as long as possible, while Gayling's 5./1. GDR and 1./1. GDR under Rittmeister von Rheinbaben withdrew to Les Hayottes. As 4./1. GDR prepared to pull back, Holzing-Berstett rode out west from La Clottée to reconnoitre and saw the led horses of B Sqn 18th Hussars and the troop that was guarding them diagonally to his right front. He did not see the other three troops of B Sqn as they were in dead ground from his perspective, being hidden by a low railway embankment. Nevertheless, he realized that an attack from this direction would cut off 3./1. GDR before they could get back to their horses and retire on Les Hayottes. He therefore ordered 4./1. GDR to charge the 18th Hussars' horses and horse-holders, thinking that an entire British squadron was assembled there (Poseck 1921: 99).

The German dragoons immediately obeyed his orders and galloped towards Sopper's position. As they mounted the railway embankment, however, they saw the other three troops of the 18th Hussars on foot some 300yd (274m) away to their left front. The German squadron commander immediately perceived that these dismounted cavalrymen constituted the real threat to the withdrawal of 3./1. GDR and obeying the spirit of Holzing-

Yeomanry of the Queen's Own Oxfordshire Hussars on active service in France, August or September 1914. This Yeomanry regiment was the first to join the BEF in France and took part in the battle of the Marne and the subsequent advance to the Aisne River. (DEA/BIBLIOTECA AMBROSIANA/Getty Images)

Berstett's orders, he swung 4./1. GDR obliquely to its left in order to charge the troops under Leveson. The British squadron commander had just been told of the advancing Germans by his scouts and had ordered the three troops with him, about 30 men, to wheel to their left front in an extended line when the 60-odd German dragoons topped the railway embankment. By the time the British hussars had moved into position the Germans were no more than 200yd (183m) from them, approaching at the gallop, meaning they would be on the British line within 30 seconds. The British cavalrymen immediately opened rapid fire on the charging dragoons. The effect was devastating. The British eyewitness accounts state, almost in a tone of awe, how the German squadron simply disappeared as if the ground had swallowed them up (Burnett 1922; de Lisle 1939). There was a solid line of some 30–35 dead and wounded German cavalrymen and their horses about 50yd (46m) from the British position, and the field over which the Germans had charged was scattered with more casualties. The 2nd Cavalry Brigade commander, who watched the fight from a haystack just north of Le Montcel, counted only 13 Germans from 4./1. GDR who managed to retreat to Les Hayottes (de Lisle 1939: 138). The 18th Hussars suffered no casualties.

Leveson ordered his men up to the railway embankment, where they formed a firing line among the dead and wounded Germans. To cover the rapidly retreating survivors of 4./1. GDR, another squadron of German dragoons emerged from Les Hayottes and made a half-hearted demonstration towards the British position, but without coming closer than 400yd (366m). The British artillery began to shell the German position, but without causing too much damage (Poseck 1921: 99). Leveson then ordered two men from each section to leave the firing line and provide succour to the numerous wounded Germans lying nearby (Burnett 1922). Having done what they could for the wounded, and being in an exposed position, at about 1000hrs B Sqn 18th Hussars pulled back towards Le Montcel. Under a flag of truce, the Germans requested permission to collect their wounded (Vaughan 1954: 166). This was granted and it took them over an hour to do so (de Lisle 1939: 139).

Shortly before 1000hrs the British 1st Cavalry Division received orders from GHQ not to advance until further orders were received. The advance was only resumed at midday, allowing the Garde-Kavallerie-Division to break contact and withdraw across the Petit Morin unmolested. The division's gallant flank guard, the 1. Garde-Dragoner-Regiment, paid a high price with 56 acknowledged casualties.

Analysis

CASTEAU

Although the action at Casteau was a small affair, it nevertheless highlights a number of factors that were relevant whenever the British and German cavalry clashed. The British cavalrymen were more aggressive than their German opponents, partly because they were regular soldiers while the Germans were conscripts, and partly because they had confidence in their weapons and in their ability to handle them, whereas the Germans, with less training and a shorter time served, were less skilled in weapon-handling, whether it be the lance or the rifle. The Germans compounded these disadvantages by not being as good cross-country riders as the British, despite being excellent *manège* horsemen. Indeed, the German cavalry tended to confine itself to moving along roads and avoided cross-country movement (Poseck 1921: 213). In short, the British, being regular soldiers, were better trained and more self-confident than the Germans and, therefore, had an advantage every time the opposing cavalry forces met in combat.

This better training is also seen in the difference between the British and German methods of scouting. The German reconnaissance patrol came straight down the main Mons–Brussels road with little attempt at concealment. The German cavalrymen were also moving fairly quickly, having taken just over an hour to cover the 6 miles (10km) between Soignies and the Saint-Denis crossroads, which implies that they were not being as careful as they might. By contrast, Major Bridges took his squadron into the sheltered valley north of Saint-Denis and sent out his patrols covertly from there. Moreover, when C Sqn did advance down the main road as contact squadron, the British cavalrymen took 30 minutes to move 1¼ miles (2km), implying that they were being cautious and deliberate. Consequently, British reconnaissance was far more effective than German. Within hours of arriving at Mons British cavalry scouts had identified that there was a division of

German cavalry at Soignies and had also ascertained a good approximation of the total strength and direction of movement of the 1. Armee as it marched from Brussels. By contrast, the Germans had no idea that the BEF was even in Belgium and, even after the encounter at Casteau, could only report that they had met British cavalry. To the credit of Leutnant Hoensbroech's *Zug*, however, he did resume his reconnaissance patrol once C Sqn 4th Dragoon Guards had withdrawn and was able to establish that British infantry were also present along the Mons–Condé Canal.

CERIZY–MOŸ

This small action between the 5th Cavalry Brigade and the 3. Garde-Kavallerie-Brigade highlights a number of lessons. German reconnaissance was not very effective and failed to detect the presence of a complete brigade of British cavalry barring its way. It was because Oberst von Senden wrongly believed that he was facing scattered and weak forces that he ordered a mounted attack. The German tactics of pushing out dismounted squadrons on the flanks, supported by artillery, while the centre carried out a mounted charge, would have made sense if the flanking squadrons had been in a position to support the charge with fire to suppress the British defences. It seems, however, that Senden's intention was that the dismounted squadrons were to cover the flanks, rather than support the mounted squadrons. This may explain why Batterie Graf Roedern thought it more important to shell the 20th Hussars rather than to engage in counter-battery fire to suppress J Bty RHA.

It is difficult to justify the German squadron commanders' decision to dismount on an exposed slope under heavy and accurate enemy fire; nevertheless, when the German dragoons found themselves in this perilous situation, they conducted themselves admirably. They managed a difficult withdrawal while maintaining a steady and accurate fire on the troops opposing them. Had the soldiers of Leutnant von Schwerin's *Zug* received the order to retire to their horses at La Folie Farm along with the rest of 4./1. GDR, German casualties would have been minimal. If the German cavalry had employed the British cavalry practice of bringing the led horses forward to the men instead of expecting the men to retire on foot to their horses, Schwerin's *Zug* would not have been left behind. Nevertheless, even when caught by a surprise mounted attack on their flank, the dragoons responded very quickly and fought most valiantly, as the British acknowledged.

Had the Garde-Schützen-Bataillon come into action against the British cavalry, things might have ended rather differently, and the British must have suffered far higher casualties. It was by a combination of luck and professional intuition that the shellfire from J Bty RHA hit the German assembly area and disrupted

A German cavalry scout in the Somme region. Reconnaissance was the fundamental cavalry role in 1914. The German cavalry tended to rely on officers' patrols to carry out the close-in scouting required to obtain accurate information about the enemy. It seems, however, that the officers were not adequately trained for the task and German reconnaissance was, therefore, not of as high a standard as might be desired by senior commanders reliant on information brought in by their cavalry patrols. (Bettmann/Getty Images)

their advance. The war diary of J Bty RHA records that Brigadier-General Chetwode acknowledged that his brigade might have been in some difficulty but for the battery's effective supporting fire.

From the British perspective, the day's combat offered a conclusive vindication of pre-war doctrine and training. The 12th Lancers provided a textbook demonstration of combined shock and fire action, as well as cooperation between cavalry and artillery. The 20th Hussars, already weakened by having one squadron detached, contemplated a similar attack with combined fire and shock action, but had too few men available to make this viable. It is easy to imagine the complete destruction of Lieutenant Sparrow's troop if it had attempted a mounted charge on Batterie Graf Roedern, supported as it was by two dismounted squadrons of dragoons. Fortunately for the British, Lieutenant-Colonel Graham Edwards, CO 20th Hussars, realized its impracticability and countermanded his original order for a mounted attack. In terms of morale, the day's action gave a much-needed boost to the 5th Cavalry Brigade and, indeed, to the BEF as a whole, especially as it was engaged in that most demoralizing of military manoeuvres – a prolonged retreat. The British were convinced that they had rendered the 3. Garde-Kavallerie-Brigade combat ineffective and had considerably dampened German morale. The German accounts do not bear this out, however, and the actions of the 3. Garde-Kavallerie-Brigade ten days later at Le Montcel demonstrated that the German dragoons had lost none of their élan or eagerness for mounted combat.

British cavalry scouts. After their bitter experience in the Second Anglo-Boer War, the British cavalry spent a great deal of time learning how to scout. This was especially the case when Major-General Robert Baden-Powell was appointed Inspector of Cavalry in 1903. His book, *Aids to Scouting for N.C.O's & Men*, was widely studied by cavalrymen around the world; it became a best-seller and helped to launch the Boy Scout Movement. (Photo by: Universal History Archive/ Universal Images Group via Getty Images)

LE MONTCEL

As the initial contact between the British and German cavalry forces on 7 September consisted of a series of independent skirmishes between small patrols and outposts, the course of the fighting was confused and cavalrymen from one side or the other often found themselves unexpectedly separated from their own forces and isolated in the midst of the enemy. This makes it difficult to give a detailed account of these initial skirmishes. What does seem to have happened is that small parties of British and Germans chased each other in and out of Le Montcel at least a couple of times each. This independent combat between small, dispersed bodies of men was not envisaged in pre-war doctrine or training, and individual accounts by participants in the fighting reflect the confusion and uncertainty of events. Nevertheless, junior commanders on both sides appear to have used their own initiative to seize opportunities to strike at the enemy; the actions of Lieutenant Taylor-Whitehead and Sergeant Mehlis being cases in point.

A German cavalryman lies dead by his horse, 1914. On a number of occasions, the German cavalry suffered very high casualties when it attempted to launch mounted attacks against dismounted enemy units armed with modern rifles and machine guns. It took brigade and regimental commanders some time to acknowledge that the massed cavalry charges practised at the *Kaisermanöver* before World War I were no longer practicable in the face of modern firepower and that the cavalry's best opportunities for charging home with the *arme blanche* were in small-unit actions at squadron or troop level. (Universal History Archive/Universal Images Group via Getty Images)

In both the mounted charge and the mêlée, it is easy to assume that each man was totally focused on riding down the enemy cavalryman right before him. The total casualties from the fight, however, would seem to indicate that this was not the case. In the charge and mêlée, the 9th Lancers suffered one man killed, Private Arthur Bryer, and nine wounded, including the CO and adjutant, along with eight horses killed. The 1. Garde-Dragoner-Regiment recorded 17 dragoons wounded, of whom 13 were captured. In addition, one unwounded German hiding in the orchard was also captured (Coleman 1916: 97). The British eyewitness accounts definitely state that a number of Germans were killed. Frederic Coleman (1916: 98), who wandered over the combat site shortly after the fight to break the *Stahlrohrlanzen* lying scattered next to the German casualties, discovered that not all of these were dead, but does not indicate that there were no dead Germans at all. The number of deaths is not recorded in the German accounts, although Poseck (1921: 99) simply remarks that the Germans who died in the fight had not done so in vain. Calculating the number of German dead is problematic. If the 5./1. GDR ratio of wounded to killed was the same as the 9th Lancers', then they had only two men killed; or assuming that their casualties reflected the ratio of three wounded for every man killed, which is the average in 20th-century conflicts, then between five and six dragoons died. Nevertheless, what is surprising is that there were so few fatalities inflicted by the *arme blanche* in a cavalry combat involving over 150 men. Perhaps the most salutary lesson, therefore, was the annihilation of 4./1. GDR by dismounted rifle fire from B Sqn 18th Hussars. It was, after all, the men of the 18th Hussars who inflicted by far the greater number of casualties on the Germans and at no cost to themselves.

After the action, the Germans were convinced that the British pursuit was stopped by the blow they had received from 5./1. GDR at Le Montcel (Poseck 1921: 99). For their part, the British were sure that they had given the enemy a severe mauling and that they had been shown to be the better cavalry in lance-to-lance combat, inflicting more casualties on the Germans than they themselves received. Both sides believed, incorrectly, that they had rendered the enemy unit combat ineffective as a result of the fight.

Aftermath

With the development of trench warfare in western Europe from October 1914 onwards the opportunities for cavalry to perform their traditional roles as mobile troops were severely curtailed. In eastern Europe the Germans still employed cavalry, but it was quickly recognized that the mounted combat in large formations for which the German cavalry was trained, was no longer practicable on the modern battlefield, making the retention of large numbers of mounted men unnecessary. The German Army urgently needed trained soldiers in the trenches, and the cavalry divisions were an obvious pool of manpower. Moreover, by 1916 Germany began to experience a shortage of horses and supplying the artillery was a priority. In October 1916, therefore, the 3. Kavallerie-Division was disbanded, while the 4., 5. and 9. Kavallerie-Divisionen were 'dismounted', i.e. converted into light infantry as *Kavallerie-Schützen* divisions. In November 1917, the 6. and 7. Kavallerie-Divisionen were dismounted, followed by the prestigious Garde-

Helmet-clad British cavalry move across a water obstacle and up a steep slope. Field Marshal Sir Douglas Haig insisted on retaining large numbers of cavalry on the Western Front, much to the displeasure of Prime Minister David Lloyd George and other politicians at home. Haig was correct, however, as the cavalry constituted his only mobile force and, when the trench deadlock was finally broken in 1918 and the fighting moved into open terrain, the cavalry was once again able to demonstrate its utility as a mobile arm capable of manoeuvring in all kinds of terrain. (Photo12/ Universal Images Group via Getty Images)

German divisional cavalry pass by captured British trenches. In the trench deadlock on the Western Front, the opportunities for divisional cavalry to carry out its traditional roles of reconnaissance, screening its own forces, or pursuing a defeated enemy were seldom possible. The deep and complex network of trenches and the muddy ground, stripped bare and smashed up by artillery bombardment, denied cavalry its most important asset, its mobility. Many soldiers (and politicians) concluded, therefore, that the cavalry was obsolete. This conclusion, drawn from the abnormal conditions of trench warfare, was shown to be false whenever cavalry could exploit its mobility, as in Palestine in 1917–18 and in the Allied advance into Germany in 1918. (Bettmann/ Getty Images)

Kavallerie-Division in March 1918 (Cron 2001: 104*f*). In 1914 the cavalry was the most eminent and influential arm in the Imperial German Army and on mobilization it numbered over 100,000 men in 146 regiments. By the armistice in November 1918 about 60 regiments (250 squadrons) were serving as divisional cavalry attached to infantry divisions, while of the original 110 active-service regiments only 22 were still mounted and serving as cavalry; the rest had either been disbanded or converted into *Kavallerie-Schützen* regiments (Nash 1980: 52–53; Cron 2001: 130). The divisional cavalry was seldom employed in scouting, its traditional cavalry role, being used instead to provide escorts for the divisional commander or orderlies and despatch riders for subordinate commanders within the division.

The British, on the other hand, retained a cavalry corps on the Western Front, despite political pressure to dismount these regiments. Field Marshal Sir Douglas Haig, himself a cavalryman, fully understood that the BEF needed to have a mobile force at hand to exploit any breakthrough in the German defences. When the trench deadlock was finally broken in 1918 the British cavalry were, thus, able to fulfil the arm's traditional roles as mobile troops (Kenyon 2011). Moreover, the British were able to draw upon the superb horsemen of Australia, Canada, New Zealand and South Africa, all of whom were primarily trained as mounted riflemen. The Canadians served on the Western Front. The South Africans served in German East Africa, but harsh conditions and endemic diseases prevented any noteworthy use of the mounted arm. In Palestine, however, the ANZAC (Australian and New Zealand Army Corps) mounted riflemen, British Yeomanry and Indian cavalry showed what could be achieved. Under the command of Field Marshal Sir Edmund Allenby, the British and Imperial troops drove the Ottoman and German forces out of Palestine, Transjordan, Lebanon and Syria. This campaign exemplified the correct use of the mounted arm in attack, outflanking the enemy, and pursuit and fully answered those sceptics who wished to abolish the horsed cavalry as obsolete and ineffectual (Wavell 1929).

UNIT ORGANIZATIONS

German

On mobilization the German Army fielded a total of 146 cavalry regiments, made up of 110 active-service, 33 Reserve, two Landwehr and one Ersatz (replacement) regiment. While the majority of these regiments were split up among the army corps as divisional cavalry to the infantry, 66 regiments were grouped together into 33 cavalry brigades, which were in turn formed into 11 cavalry divisions. One cavalry division was sent to the East to face the Russians, while the remaining ten were grouped into four cavalry corps for service in the West. To reflect the fact that these cavalry corps did not have the equivalent supporting troops or command staff structure of an infantry army corps, each was designated *Höherer Kavallerie-Kommandeur* (HKK), i.e. 'Higher Cavalry Commander' (Cron 2001: 94). In order to supplement the firepower of the cavalry, each HKK also had a number of *Jäger* or *Schützen* battalions attached to it, which were allocated to the cavalry divisions as required. Each *Kavallerie-Division* was made up of three brigades of two regiments each, as well as various attached troops, such as signallers, pioneers and an *Artillerie-Abtheilung* that consisted of three batteries, each with six 7.7cm field guns.

Each active-service regiment had five squadrons, one of which remained in barracks in Germany as a training and administrative squadron. Hence the regiments deployed with four sabre squadrons each. The war establishment of a four-squadron active-service regiment was 36 officers, 688 other ranks, 709 remounts, and 60 draught horses to pull two bridging wagons, one telephone wagon, one medical wagon, five fodder wagons, five supply wagons and five baggage wagons (Nash 1980: 52). Each squadron consisted of four *Züge* (platoons). Each *Zug* had one officer and 22–24 other ranks.

The *Jäger* battalions fielded four rifle companies, each with five officers, 259 other ranks, ten horses and four wagons. In addition, each battalion also had a *Radfahr-Compagnie* of three officers and 124 other ranks mounted on bicycles; a machine-gun company with four officers, 95 men, six machine guns, 87 horses and 15 wagons; a support train of 30 men, 74 horses, eight ammunition wagons, four field kitchens and ten baggage wagons; and a ten-lorry *Jäger-Kraftwagen-Kolonne* (Nash 1980: 40–43).

British

The British sent five cavalry brigades to France with the BEF. The 1st to 4th Cavalry brigades were grouped together in the Cavalry Division under the command of Major-General Sir Edmund Allenby, while the 5th Cavalry Brigade was an independent formation under Brigadier-General Sir Philip Chetwode. Senior cavalrymen acknowledged that a four-brigade division was too large to be handled effectively in the field but had accepted it as the best way to save cavalry regiments from being disbanded by a parsimonious Treasury (Vaughan 1954: 161). In September 1914, therefore, the 3rd Cavalry Brigade was detached from the Cavalry Division and combined with the 5th Cavalry Brigade to become the 2nd Cavalry Division, the original Cavalry Division being redesignated as the 1st Cavalry Division.

Each cavalry brigade consisted of three regiments and, from early in the campaign, an attached Royal Horse Artillery battery of six quick-firing 13-pdr guns. In addition to the cavalry divisions there were cavalry squadrons attached to the infantry as divisional cavalry. As with the German Army, the squadrons attached to the infantry divisions were not always well employed and their strength was frittered away on non-essential tasks (Vaughan 1954: 161).

The war establishment of a cavalry regiment was 26 officers, 514 other ranks, 518 remounts, 54 draught horses, six packhorses for the regimental scouts, two machine guns, 11 wagons, two carts and 15 bicycles. Each regiment consisted of three sabre squadrons of four troops each. Each troop at full strength had one officer and 32 other ranks, divided into four sections of up to eight men, each under an NCO.

The British Army was never up to full strength during peace as it was a volunteer force. On the outbreak of war, therefore, each regiment had to be brought up to full wartime establishment by recalling reservists to the Colours. In some regiments the reservists made up as much as half of the manpower. It is a tribute to the discipline and morale of the British cavalry that the absorption of reservists into regular regiments caused so little friction, and that the reservists were brought up to the necessary standards of efficiency within a fortnight of re-joining their regiments.

BIBLIOGRAPHY

War diaries

9. Kavallerie-Division (BA RH 18/2823)

13. Kavallerie-Brigade (BA MSg 2/4902)

1st Cavalry Division HQ Staff War Diary (TNA WO 95/1096/1)

2nd Cavalry Brigade HQ (TNA WO 95/1110/1)

2nd Dragoons (Royal Scots Greys) (TNA WO 95/1139/3)

4th (Royal Irish) Dragoon Guards (TNA WO 95/1112/1)

5th Cavalry Brigade HQ (TNA WO 95/1138/1)

9th (Queen's Royal) Lancers (TNA WO 95/1113/2)

12th (Prince of Wales's Royal) Lancers (TNA WO 95/1140/1)

18th (Queen Mary's Own) Hussars (TNA WO 95/1113/1)

20th Hussars (TNA WO 95/1140/2)

Garde-Kavallerie-Division (BA RH 18/2529)

I Battery Royal Horse Artillery (TNA WO 95/1108/2)

J Battery Royal Horse Artillery (TNA WO 95/1135/2)

Kürassier-Regiment 4 (BA PH 11II/3)

Personal diaries

Dyer, Pte H. (1914). Personal Diary, 4th Dragoon Guards. York Army Museum.

Wright, Captain A. (1914). Personal Diary, 4th Dragoon Guards. York Army Museum.

Published sources

Anglesey, Marquess of (1996). *A History of the British Cavalry 1816–1919, Vol. 7: The Curragh Incident and the Western Front, 1914.* London: Leo Cooper.

Ascoli, D. (2001). *The Mons Star: The British Expeditionary Force 1914.* Edinburgh: Birlinn.

Badsey, S. (2008). *Doctrine and Reform in the British Cavalry 1880–1918.* Aldershot: Ashgate.

Barrow, G. (1942). *The Fire of Life.* London: Hutchinson.

Bernhardi, F., trans. C.S. Goldman (1909). *Cavalry in Future Wars*, 2nd edition. London: John Murray.

Bernhardi, F., trans. Major G.T.M. Bridges DSO (1910). *Cavalry in War and Peace.* London: Hugh Rees.

Bridges, G.T.M. (1938). *Alarms and Excursions: Reminiscences of a Soldier.* London: Longmans Green & Co.

Burnett, C. (1922). 'A Cavalry Episode in the Advance to the Marne', in *The Cavalry Journal*, July 1922.

Coleman, F. (1916). *From Mons to Ypres with French.* London: Sampson Low, Marston & Co.

Cooksey, J. & Murland, J. (2014). *The Retreat from Mons 1914: North – Casteau to Le Cateau.* Barnsley: Pen & Sword.

Creagh, O'M. (1915). 'Notes on Experience Gained at the Front' in J. Solano, ed., *Musketry (.303 and .22 Cartridges).* London: John Murray: pp. vi–xii.

Cron, H., trans. Wolton (2001). *Imperial German Army 1914–1918.* Solihull: Helion.

De Lisle, B. (1939). *Reminiscences of Sport and War.* London: Eyre & Spottiswoode.

Felton, W.S. (1962). *Masters of Equitation.* London: J.A. Allen & Co.

French, E.G. (1951). *Good-Bye to Boot and Saddle or The Tragic Passing of British Cavalry.* London: Hutchinson & Co.

Gayling von Altheim, C. (1920). *Das 1. Garde-Dragoner-Regiment im Kriege 1914–1918.* Berlin: Kyffhäuser.

Geßler, H. von (1927). *Die 2. Garde-Dragoner im Weltkriege 1914–1918.* Oldenburg: Stalling.

Gibb, H. (1925). *Record of the 4th Royal Irish Dragoon Guards in the Great War 1914–1918.* Canterbury: No Publisher.

Gilby, T., ed. (1953). *Britain at Arms.* London: Eyre & Spottiswoode.

Glasmeier, H. (1932). *Geschichte des Kürassier-Regiments von Driesen-Westfalen-Nr. 4.* Oldenburg: Stalling Verlag.

Holmes, R. (1996). *Riding the Retreat: Mons to the Marne - 1914 Revisited.* London: Pimlico.

Home, A. & Briscoe, D., ed. (1985). *The Diary of a World War I Cavalry Officer.* Tunbridge Wells: Costello.

Howard-Vyse, R.G.H. (1921). 'The Fifth Cavalry Brigade at Cerizy, August 28, 1914', in *The Cavalry Journal*, April 1921.

Humphries, M.O. & Maker, J., eds (2013). *Germany's Western Front: Translations from the German Official History of the Great War*. Ontario: Wilfred Laurier University Press.

Kenyon, D. (2011). *Horsemen in No Man's Land: British Cavalry and Trench Warfare 1914–1918*. Barnsley: Pen & Sword.

Maitland, F.H. (1951). *Hussar of the Line*. London: Hurst & Blackett.

Maurice, F. (1921). *Forty Days in 1914*. 2nd edition. London: Constable.

Maze, P. (1934). *A Frenchman in Khaki*. London: Heinemann.

Müller, F. (1922). *Brandenburgisches Jäger-Bataillon Nr. 3*. Oldenburg: Stalling.

Nash, D.B. (1980). *Imperial German Army Handbook 1914–1918*. London: Ian Allan.

Norman, ed. (1938). *Kriegskamerad Pferd*. Berlin: Wilhelm Limpert-Verlag.

Osburn, A. (1932). *Unwilling Passenger*. London: Faber & Faber.

Pegler, M. (2012). *The Lee-Enfield Rifle*. Weapon 17. Oxford: Osprey Publishing.

Pitman, T.T. (1923). 'General Outline of Cavalry Operations on the Western Front', in *The Cavalry Journal*, Vol. 13.

Poseck, M. (1921). *Die deutsche Kavallerie 1914 in Belgien und Frankreich*. Berlin: Mittler.

Roberts, F. (1903). 'Cavalry Armament', in *The Journal of The Royal United Services Institute* 47: 575–82.

Satter, A. (2004). *Die deutsche Kavallerie im Ersten Weltkrieg*. Norderstedt: Books on Demand GmbH.

Tackle, P. (2006). *The Affair at Nery 1 September 1914*. Barnsley: Pen & Sword.

Terraine, J. (1972). *Mons: The Retreat to Victory*. London: Pan.

Thomas, E. (1939). 'I Fired the First Shot!', in Hammerton, J., ed., *The Great War: I Was There! Part 1*: pp. 41–42.

Tylden, G. (1965). *Horses and Saddlery*. London: J.A. Allen & Co.

Van Emden, R., ed. (1996). *Tickled to Death to Go: Memoirs of a Cavalryman in the First World War*. Staplehurst: Spellmount.

Vaughan, J. (1954). *Cavalry and Sporting Memories*. Bala: The Bala Press.

Vogel, J. (1916). *3000 kilometer mit der Garde-Kavallerie*. Bielefeld: Velhagen & Klasing.

von der Marwitz, G. (1921). 'Die deutsche Kavallerie 1914', in *Militar-Wochenblatt*, 105.50: 1.

Watson, P. (2016). *Centenary of the Last Charges of the 9th/12th Lancers (Prince of Wales's)*. Kettering: Crest Publications.

Watson, P. (2019). *Audregnies*. Solihull: Helion.

Wavell, A.P. (1929). *The Palestine Campaigns*. 2nd edition. London: Constable.

Westecker, W. (1939). *Westfalen stand wie ein Fels. Die westfälischen Regimenter im Weltkrieg 1914 bis 1918*. Dortmund: Westfalen-Verlag.

Military manuals

Bohlen und Halbach, H. (1912). *Felddienst-Instruktionen zum Gebrauch für den Kavallerie-Unteroffizier*. Berlin: Eisenschmidt.

Gall, H.R. (1908). *Tactical Questions and Answers on Cavalry Training 1907*. London: Forster Groom.

Kriegsministerium (1909). *Exerzier-Reglement für die Kavallerie 1909*. Berlin: Mittler.

Kriegsministerium (1912). *Reitvorschrift 1912*. Berlin: Mittler.

Pelet-Narbonne, G. (1911). *von Mirus' Leitfaden für den Kavalleristen bei seinem Verhalten in und außer dem Dienste*. Berlin: Mittler.

Oberbefehlshaber des Heeres (1937). *H.Dv. 12 Reitvorschrift*. Berlin: Mittler.

Unger, K. (1912). *Drei Jahre im Sattel: Ein Lern- und Lesebuch für den Dienstunterricht des Deutschen Kavalleristen*. Berlin: Liebelschen.

War Office (1907). *Field Service Manual: Cavalry Regiment*. London: HMSO.

War Office (1908). *Animal Management 1908*. London: HMSO.

War Office (1912). *Cavalry Training 1912*. London: HMSO.

War Office (1912). *Yeomanry and Mounted Rifle Training, Parts I & II 1912*. London: HMSO.

War Office (1913). *Field Service Pocket Book*. London: HMSO.

INDEX

References to illustrations are shown in **bold**. References to plates are shown in bold with caption pages in brackets, e.g. **64–65**, (66).